A CENTURY OF STRUGGLE IN DELGANY AND KILCOOLE

Maynooth Studies in Irish Local History

SERIES EDITOR   Raymond Gillespie

This is one of six new pamphlets in the Maynooth Studies in Irish Local History Series to be published in the year 2000. Like their predecessors, most of the pamphlets are based on theses completed as part of the M.A. in local history programme in National University of Ireland, Maynooth. While the regions and time span which they cover are diverse, from Waterford to Monaghan, and from the fourteenth to the twentieth centuries, they all share a conviction that the exploration of the local past can shed light on the evolution of modern societies. They each demonstrate that understanding the evolution of local societies is important. The local worlds of Ireland in the past are as complex and sophisticated as the national framework in which they are set. The communities which peopled those local worlds, whether they be the inhabitants of religious houses, industrial villages or rural parishes, shaped and were shaped by their environments to create a series of interlocking worlds of considerable complexity. Those past worlds are best interpreted not through local administrative divisions, such as the county, but in human units: local places where communities of people lived and died. Untangling what held these communities together, and what drove them apart, gives us new insights into the world we have lost.

These pamphlets each make a significant contribution to understanding Irish society in the past. Together with twenty-eight earlier works in this series they explore something of the hopes and fears of those who lived in Irish local communities in the past. In doing so they provide examples of the practice of local history at its best and show the vibrant discipline which the study of local history in Ireland has become in recent years.

Maynooth Studies in Irish Local History: Number 34

A century of struggle in Delgany and Kilcoole

An exploration of the social implications of population change in north-east Wicklow, 1666–1779

Brian Gurrin

IRISH ACADEMIC PRESS
DUBLIN • PORTLAND, OR

First published in 2000 by
IRISH ACADEMIC PRESS
44, Northumberland Road, Dublin 4, Ireland
and in the United States of America by
IRISH ACADEMIC PRESS
c/o ISBS, 5804 NE Hassalo Street, Portland, OR 97213–3644.

website: www.iap.ie

British Library Cataloguing in Publication Data
Gurrin, Brian
    A century of struggle in Delgany and Kilcoole : an exploration of the social
implications of population change in north east Wicklow, 1666–1779. –
(Maynooth studies in Irish local history; no. 34)
    1. Delgany (Ireland) – Population – History – 17th century 2. Kilcoole (Ireland)
– Population – History – 17th century 3. Delgany (Ireland) – Population –
History – 18th century 4. Kilcoole (Ireland) – Population – History – 18th
century
    I. Title
    304.6'094184
    ISBN 0–7165–2723–5

Library of Congress Cataloging-in-Publication Data
Gurrin, Brian, 1968–
    A century of struggle in Delgany and Kilcoole : an exploration of the social
implications of population change in north-east Wicklow, 1666–1779 / Brian
Gurrin.
    p. cm.—(Maynooth studies in local history; no. 34)
    ISBN 0–7165–2723–5 (pbk)
    1. Wicklow (Ireland : County)—Population—History. 2. Delgany (Ireland)—
Population—History. 3. Kilcoole (Ireland)—Population—History. 4. Ireland—
Population—History—17th century. 5. Ireland—Population—History—18th
century. I. Title. II. Series.

HB3590.W53 G87 2000
304.6'09418'4—dc21   00–044840

Typeset in 10 pt on 12 pt Bembo by
Carrigboy Typesetting Services, County Cork
Printed by ColourBooks Ltd., Dublin

Contents

Preface

I would like to express my thanks to the many people who assisted me during the course of my study. Firstly, I would like to thank Dr Raymond Gillespie for his remarkable patience, assistance, encouragement and his invaluable support over the past number of years. I would also like to thank Rev. Nigel Waugh, rector of Delgany parish, who regularly granted me access to the Delgany parish registers at short notice and without whose help I could not have completed this study. Thanks are also due to the staff of the National Library of Ireland who went to great lengths to source and acquire manuscripts for me. Also, the staff of Bray, Greystones and St Patrick's College, Maynooth libraries were most helpful in providing me with useful information as were Dr Raymond Refaussé and Mrs Heather Smith in the R.C.B. library. Finally, thank you to Mary, Niamh and Seán for your patience, tolerance and forbearance in allowing me the time and space to complete my studies. I hope you are happy with the result.

NOTE ON TERMINOLOGY

The Delgany union was comprised of the ecclesiastical parishes of Delgany, Kilcoole and Kilmacanoge and is variously termed the Delgany area, the Delgany parishes, the Delgany region and Delgany in this pamphlet. The Bray union was comprised of the parish of Bray in County Wicklow and the Dublin parishes of Oldconnaught and Kiltiernan.

Introduction

Wicklow is a maritime county located on the eastern seaboard of Ireland, immediately to the south of County Dublin. Physically and geologically the county is something of an oddity in the province of Leinster and indeed in the island as a whole as no other county has as great a proportion of upland and mountainous land. A massive elevated granite tract runs from the southern coast of Dublin Bay in a south-westerly direction through the heart of the county to the Derry River near the Wexford border. These mountains have tended to divide the county in two and historically communication between the flat and fertile east and the west was difficult. Neville's mid-eighteenth century map of the county clearly shows the few crossing points that existed at that time.[1]

Of all the various regions in Wicklow, the north-eastern corner of the county has been subject to the most diverse influences. Following the arrival of Norman power in Ireland, the region was on the route linking the capital with the Norman south-east. Castles were constructed in the twelfth century at Bray[2] and by 1213 at Newcastle[3] to protect the important north-south route. As English power contracted in the fifteenth and sixteenth centuries north-east Wicklow's frontier situation was confirmed as it became a bulwark against attacks by the Gaelic Irish. More castles were constructed at Rathdown[4] and further inland at Powerscourt and Fassaroe to protect English lands from attack by the O'Byrne and O'Toole clans who had based themselves in the Wicklow Mountains. Despite bordering County Dublin, Wicklow was the last county to be shired – as late as 1608.[5]

In the eighteenth and nineteenth centuries Wicklow became an important tourist location and the principal roads from Dublin passed through north-east Wicklow at Bray and Enniskerry. The area was within easy reach of Dublin and yet was largely rural. In 1669 there were only ten hearth tax payees in the town of Delgany while the nearest urban areas were the small town of Bray to the north and the larger town of Wicklow to the south.[6] The area was also quite remote as the main road to Wexford did not pass through Bray but via the Scalp to Enniskerry, a few miles to the west.

The soil in the area is generally fertile and easily worked. In the early nineteenth century Radcliffe reported that the land 'of an apparently light quality, is known to produce crops equal, if not superior to those on the richest soils in other parts of Ireland'.[7] This soil is conducive to tillage farming and the area was a grain-producing region at least as far back as the early seventeenth century.[8] In 1784 Wilson refers to the northern part of the Glen of the Downs, effectively the parish of Kilmacanoge, as being 'chiefly under Corn'[9] whereas in 1812 'the generality of the crops [oats] . . . extending along the coast between Bray and Arklow, are not exceeded in quantity or quality in any part of Ireland'.[10] The Dublin Society survey of County Wicklow speaks of 'sixteen or eighteen crops of corn following, without interposing anything but grain crops'[11] in the Newtownmountkennedy area in the late eighteenth century.

The aim of this pamphlet is to study population change in the parishes of the Delgany union between 1666 and 1779. It will be seen that in the early seventeenth century the Protestant congregations in north-east Wicklow were, with just a single exception, very small and many of the churches were in a state of decay.[12] The creation of unions of parishes thus became a practical necessity and the Delgany union, comprising the Church of Ireland parishes of Delgany, Kilcoole and Kilmacanoge, was formed 'prior to the year 1700'.[13] Newcastle parish, although closely linked with the Delgany union, always remained an independent parish.[14]

The first chapter focuses on studying both the general population trend and also the trends in the Protestant population in the civil parishes of north-east Wicklow and south-east Dublin between the 1660s and the 1860s. In particular, periods when the population appears to have either advanced rapidly or else contracted are identified.

The principal sources used include a hearth-tax roll for County Dublin (1664)[15] and for County Wicklow (1669)[16] and a 1739 hearth-tax summary for County Wicklow.[17] Another source used is the 1766 Religious Census summary for the diocese of Dublin,[18] which includes estimates of the number of Protestant and Papist families in the unions of Bray and Delgany and the parishes of Newcastle and Powerscourt. This summary also contains estimates for the actual Protestant and Papist populations in the parish of Newcastle and the Delgany union. In the nineteenth century population and religious breakdown statistics became more widely available with the commencement of the decennial census series and the 1831 and 1861 censuses are thus used to complete the population picture.

Having determined the general population trends during this two-hundred-year period the second chapter focuses on the specifics of this change in the Delgany union and seeks to determine if there were particular 'rhythms' to life in the area during the seventeenth and eighteenth centuries. The principal sources for this chapter are the Delgany union baptism and burial registers, both of which commenced in 1666.[19] The registers are used to verify the general population trends observed in the first chapter. Key questions that are considered include whether the agricultural makeup of the area or the time of the year had any influence on the timing of conceptions. Did people plan the birth of a child for the spring months so that the child could be well nourished during the seasons of plenty? Did people try to avoid giving birth during the harvest period? Was the death rate higher during winter than during the other seasons?

The third chapter focuses on the mechanics of population change in the area paying particular attention to fertility levels. In addition, some of the key factors that typically influence population change are investigated. For instance, the average age of marriage of a woman is often cited as an important factor in population change. This chapter investigates whether there was a discernible fluctuation in the average age of marriage during the period under study which may account for general population trends. Other key indicators that are studied include the duration between marriage and the birth (baptism) of the first child and the interval between successive births. Where appropriate, the statistics and trends are compared with the general portrait of population change that was outlined in the two earlier chapters to see if they support or contradict the general trends. The timing of marriage is also studied in detail. Anne Kussmaul has argued that in early modern England marriages were planned so that they impacted as little as possible on the monetary earnings of the married couple – the groom in particular.[20] This consideration meant that marriages tended to be held when there was little work to be done. Public holidays and periods of slack following the busiest times seem to have been the most popular times for marriages. As will be seen, the main difficulty in studying the Delgany marriage records is related to the fact that just so few marriages were recorded. Nonetheless the marriage patterns in the area are examined to see if they exhibit any of the trends that Kussmaul identified in English parishes and some interesting results are observed.

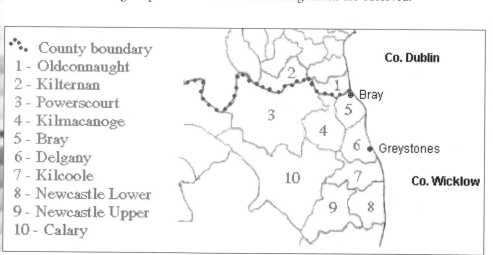

- County boundary
- 1 - Oldconnaught
- 2 - Kilternan
- 3 - Powerscourt
- 4 - Kilmacanoge
- 5 - Bray
- 6 - Delgany
- 7 - Kilcoole
- 8 - Newcastle Lower
- 9 - Newcastle Upper
- 10 - Calary

Location map of the parishes of north-east Wicklow

General population trends in the north-east Wicklow area between 1660 and 1861

'This Barony [Half Rathdown] is not very well Inhabited occasioned partly by the Roughness of the Country and partly by the destruction of the Antient Irish Inhabitants during the late warrs'[1] – late 1650s.

'Along the sea from Dublin to Bray and the town of Wicklow, for almost three or four and twenty miles, is a vein of good improved land'[2] – mid 1760s

The above quotations are illustrative of the metamorphosis that north-east Wicklow underwent in the century following the 1660 Restoration. In the aftermath of the Cromwellian Wars the coastal strip of north-east Wicklow was thinly populated and although the land was generally good and fertile the Down Survey reported that much of the forfeited lands had had 'noe improvements at all'.[3] By the 1760s, however, the population had increased substantially, the land had been improved and the area had become a significant grain and cattle producing region which was dotted with large prosperous estates. This chapter will examine the nature and extent of demographic change in north-east Wicklow between the mid-seventeenth century and the mid-nineteenth century and will aim to determine how the religious balance in the area changed during this two-hundred-year period. The principal sources that are available for conducting this population study are a 1669 hearth-money roll for County Wicklow, a hearth-money summary for County Wicklow for 1739 (and 1748), a summary of the 1766 Religious Census returns for the area and census figures on a parish basis from 1821 onwards.[4]

As the Religious Census returns for Bray are aggregated with the neighbouring Dublin parishes of Kiltiernan and Oldconnaught these two parishes will also be studied. Inclusion of these two south-east Dublin parishes is inherently sensible, however, because the parish boundaries, although clearly defined on a map, had little impact on the actual lives of the inhabitants of the area. Bray and Powerscourt parishes were bordered to the north by the parishes of Oldconnaught and Kiltiernan respectively, and travel and movement between the parishes was common.[5] Two further sources are available for these Dublin parishes – the 'census' (poll tax) of 1660 and the Dublin hearth-money roll of 1664.[6]

In 1630 the archbishop of Dublin, Launcelot Bulkeley, compiled a detailed report on the state of Protestantism in the diocese.[7] The church attendance figures in the report are particularly useful in determining the quantitative strength of Protestantism in any part of the diocese in the early seventeenth century although the report contains no indication of the general population level. In summary it can be said that Protestantism in the area was in a sorry state. Powerscourt was the only parish in the region that had a significant number of practising Protestants with a regular church attendance figure of two hundred. In stark contrast, the five parishes of Bray, Kilmacanoge, Delgany, Kilcoole and Newcastle were recorded as having only fifty practising Protestants between them while Oldconnaught and Kiltiernan had less than twenty. Only four worshipped regularly at both Delgany and Kilmacanoge, two at Kilcoole and twenty-four at Newcastle. Most of the churches in the area were reported as being in a serious state of disrepair.[8]

In the three decades following the Bulkeley report, however, the area underwent fundamental and far-reaching demographic change. Taxation lists compiled in the 1660s show that the number of Protestants in north-east Wicklow and south-east Dublin had increased substantially since Bulkeley's report had been compiled. In 1660 a poll tax was levied on the entire country that was payable by 'every person above the age of fifteen years, of either sex, of what degree or quality soever' and the figures given in the poll tax listing consequently refer to the number of adults in a townland rather than to the total population.[9] Figures are given for the total number of English and Irish (and Scottish in some counties) adults on a townland basis for virtually the entire island. It is safe to assume that 'English' and 'Irish' meant 'Protestants' and 'Catholics' respectively. Unfortunately the returns for County Wicklow appear not to have survived although Connagh (Oldconnaught) and Kiltiernan returns are available. As these figures only include persons over fifteen it is necessary to use a multiplier to convert the 'enumeration' of adults into an estimate of the total population. Cullen has suggested that a multiplier of 3 be used to convert the poll tax figures to population figures and this has been done in table 1.[10] A multiplier of 3 seems reasonable because this would approximate to six persons in an average house, a figure that many eighteenth-century commentators believed to be acceptable.[11]

Table 1 1660 poll tax return for Oldconnaught and Kiltiernan parishes

Place	Numbers as in 'poll tax'			Applying multiplier (of 3)		
	English	Irish	Total	English	Irish	Total
Connagh	10	67	77	30	201	231
Little Bray	11	15	26	33	45	78
Total Oldconnaught	21	82	103	63	246	309
Kiltiernan	2	12	14	6	36	42

It can be seen from table 1 that Protestants appear to have clustered in the quasi-urban area of Little Bray and the coastal parish of Oldconnaught. Kiltiernan, an inland parish, was more remote and more rural than Oldconnaught and seems to have been less attractive to settling Protestants. Joseph Ranson found a similar settlement pattern for the baronies of Gorey and Ballaghkeen, County Wexford in his examination of the returns for that county.[12]

Clearly there must have been inflows of Protestants into the area between 1630 and 1660 as the number of Protestants in Oldconnaught and Kiltiernan in 1660 (Bray figures not available) is more than four times the figure recorded by Bulkeley. What is important to determine at this stage is the completeness of this poll tax and whether there was a greater tendency for either Protestants or Roman Catholics to be enumerated.

Firstly, let us consider the poll tax in terms of its completeness. What the omission rate for the tax was is not known but at least some will, no doubt, have succeeded in avoiding payment. The accuracy of the figures for a particular area will thus have been influenced by, among other factors, the diligence of the tax collectors, the difficulty of the terrain and the density of the population. Kiltiernan, the more remote of the parishes, may, therefore, have had a greater payment avoidance rate than Oldconnaught. It is useful to compare the figures for Oldconnaught (including Little Bray) and Kiltiernan with the figures in the Dublin hearth money roll (1664). Thirty-two house-holders (equivalent to sixty-four adults) paid the hearth tax in Oldconnaught, ten (twenty adults) in Little Bray and six (twelve adults) in Kiltiernan. In all three cases these figures are very close to the poll tax figures, thus suggesting that either the poll tax figures are reasonably accurate or else they are equally as bad as the hearth tax figures. The latter seems the more probable as will be clear when the accuracy of the Dublin hearth tax figures is considered below.

The question of whether the tax weighed more heavily on the shoulders of Protestants or Roman Catholics is important because if either denomination was proportionately more inclined to pay the tax, then that denomination's strength will consequently be exaggerated in the population estimate. It may be assumed that both Protestant and Catholic would have wished to avoid paying the tax. However, the suspicion that Protestants may have clustered in quasi-urban areas would, if it were true, mean that they would have found it more difficult to avoid paying the tax since it is both easier and cheaper to levy a tax in a small geographic area with an above average population density – such as a small town or village – than in a rural area. Because of this Protestants would seem to have been more likely to pay the poll tax than Catholics.

Two years after the levying of this poll tax the Irish Parliament, reconstituted in the aftermath of Charles II's Restoration, passed the Hearth

Money Act of 1662.[13] This tax required an annual payment of 2s. per hearth by every qualifying household in the country. Initially exemptions from the tax were granted to three groups: houses less than a year old, buildings that were not private residences and residences where the household was dependent on alms or where the householder was a pauper.[14] In 1665 an amendment was introduced to close some loopholes in the law that had become apparent. Henceforth, hearth-tax exemptions were limited to widows who were below a certain wealth threshold and to those dependent on alms.[15] Houses with no fixed hearth were considered to have two hearths.[16] Hearth money rolls, usually from the introductory years of the tax, are extant for many parts of the country and it is most fortunate that reasonably complete hearth-money roll transcripts exist for both Dublin (1664) and Wicklow (1669).[17] Since the payees of the tax are named, it is possible to estimate the religious breakdown of the area by using surname analysis and other techniques.[18]

As the Dublin hearth money roll was compiled under the original legislation, it is probable that the level of underestimation of houses is greater than the underestimation in the Wicklow roll. It was noted earlier that the 1660 poll tax and the 1664 hearth-money roll for Dublin both show comparable figures for Oldconnaught and Kiltiernan. However, since this hearth roll inevitably underestimated the number of houses in the two parishes because of the loopholes that permitted significant numbers of people to claim exemptions, then the poll tax must likewise underestimate the total number of houses.

Furthermore, it has been suggested that the level of underestimation in early eighteenth century hearth money rolls may be of the order of 14 per cent[19] and so the exemption rate from the 1664 Dublin roll is likely to be higher because it preceded the 1665 amending legislation. A figure of 20 per cent may be closer to the correct exemption figure for this roll. There is clear evidence that some names were excluded from the Wicklow roll. For instance, a 1666 agreement between the earl of Meath and the earl of Tyrconnell lists the names of the occupiers of eight houses in Bray in that year but only one of these names appears in the hearth-money roll three years later.[20] While it is possible that, with the boundary dispute settled, the earl of Tyrconnell moved to evict the named occupiers, it seems more likely that these named tenants succeeded in avoiding paying the hearth tax. Furthermore, Protestant church records for Bray, Powerscourt and, more particularly, Delgany between 1666 and 1674 list many names that do not appear in the hearth money roll. For example, of the eighty-three householders that are recorded in the Delgany baptismal register between 1666 and 1670 inclusive, only forty-five of these persons paid hearth tax in 1669.[21] This does not, of course, mean that upwards of 45 per cent were exempt from the hearth tax.[22] However, it is clear that a 14 per cent omission rate is unlikely to be an overestimation.

As was done earlier with the poll tax returns, a multiplier representing the average number of people per house must be used to convert the hearth roll figures (enumerating household tax payees which loosely equates to houses) to population estimates. Although we cannot know for certain what this multiplier should be, a variety of sources point to 5.5 people per house being a likely figure. Most of the pre-statutory census population estimates listed by Connell[23] assumed that the average number of people occupying a house was between five and six persons. The only pre-census estimate for County Wicklow suggests that there were not 'more than five and a half to a house'[24] but this estimate is for the beginning of the nineteenth century and is a county-wide estimate.[25] A near-contemporary national estimate by William Petty also assumed that there were, on average, 5.5 people per house in 1672.[26]

Some of the surviving 1766 Religious Census data also contain both family and population estimates for various parishes. Unfortunately, however, the data for Delgany cannot be presumed to reflect family size a century earlier because, as will be seen in the next chapter, the 1760s was a decade of youthful immigration into the area after a prolonged period of population decline. The 4.63 people per house in the parishes of Delgany, Kilcoole, Kilmacanoge and Newcastle in 1766[27] can only be viewed as a transitory situation brought about by this immigration. The arrival of significant numbers of newly married couples must have temporarily reduced the average number of people per house until the stage was reached that their families were complete.[28] It is possible, however, to use the entire Census household-size data to calculate an average household-size figure for the Delgany area by applying an appropriate weighting to the various parish figures.[29] In the thesis on which this study is based this method was used and produced a reasonable figure of 5.5 people per house for the Delgany parishes. An analysis of the baptism registers also supports this figure.[30]

The earlier observation that Protestants tended to cluster in quasi-urban areas is supported by a surname analysis of the Dublin and Wicklow hearth-money rolls. All of the urban areas in the region including the towns of Bray, Enniskerry, Delgany and Kilcoole were predominantly or perhaps even exclusively Protestant.[31] Thus, as was the case with the 1660 poll tax, Protestants may be over represented in the hearth rolls but probably not by a significant amount.

If the rate of omission from the two hearth money rolls is presumed to be 20 per cent for the Dublin roll and 14 per cent for the Wicklow roll, adjusted figures for population and religious persuasion can be calculated for south-east Dublin (1664) and north-east Wicklow (1669). For convenience it is assumed that Protestants are equally likely to be omitted from the roll as Catholics even though this may slightly overestimate the relative size of the Protestant population. These adjusted figures are shown in table 2. The number of Protestant houses in each parish has been estimated by using a combination of techniques including surname analysis.[32]

Table 2 Adjusted post-Restoration population and religious breakdown
estimates for south-east Dublin and north-east Wicklow parishes
(from the hearth-money rolls of the 1660s)

Parish	Estimated no. of Prot. houses	Total no. of houses	Multiplier (5.5 people per house)		Adjusted no.of Prots.	Adjusted total pop.	Proportion Protestant
			Prot. pop.	*Total pop.*			
Bray	23	41	127	226	145	258	56.19%
Delgany	15	49	83	270	95	308	30.74%
Kilcoole	41	108	226	594	258	677	38.05%
Kilmacanoge	30	78	165	429	188	489	38.46%
Newcastle	66	164	363	902	414	1,028	40.24%
Powerscourt	51	113	281	622	320	709	45.18%
Oldconnaught	18	54	99	297	119	356	33.33%
Kiltiernan	6	17	33	94	40	113	35.11%

From table 2 it appears that Bray parish had a substantial Protestant population
in 1669 although the figure of 56 per cent Protestant seems extraordinarily
high. It may not be wildly inaccurate, however, as the Religious Census figures
also suggest that a large proportion of the parish was Protestant in the mid-
eighteenth century. The figures for Delgany and Kilcoole seem reasonably
accurate but the 39 per cent Protestant figure for Kilmacanoge far exceeds any
other estimates for the proportion of Protestants in the parish.[33]

The Protestant proportion of the parish populations shown in table 2
contrasts starkly with the numbers of worshippers that Bulkeley recorded in
1630 and indicates that substantial Protestant migration into the area must
have occurred during the middle years of the seventeenth century. As a
consequence of this immigration one would expect the age profile of the area
to be reduced and a period of high baptisms and low burials to follow as new,
young couples started raising families. It will be seen in the final chapter that
there was indeed a significant differential between baptism and burial rates in
the 1660s.

Kilcoole was the most densely populated parish in north-east Wicklow in
the 1660s while the neighbouring parishes of Newcastle, Delgany and
Powerscourt were thinly populated. Population densities on a parish by parish
basis using nineteenth century boundaries are shown in table 3.

Table 3 Estimated population density in north-east Wicklow parishes in 1669 (Area (acres) from *Census of Ireland 1861 – General report*, pp 120–2)

Parish	Area (acres)	Estimated population	No. of acres per person in 1669	Rank
Kilcoole	4,476	677	6.6	1
Kilmacanoge	5,401	489	11.0	2
Newcastle	11,776	1,028	11.5	3
Bray	2,986	258	11.6	4
Delgany	3,978	308	12.9	5
Powerscourt	18,938	709	26.7	6

Almost a century after the compiling of these hearth-money rolls parliament sanctioned the holding of a religious census in 1766 for the purpose of determining the numbers of Protestants and papists in the country. The parish ministers were directed 'to return a list of the several families in their parishes to this House [of Lords] . . . distinguishing which are Protestants and which are papists and also a list of the several reputed popish priests and friars residing in their parishes'.[34] The vast majority of these returns have since been lost and the only returns relating to the area under study are contained in a Tennison Groves compiled summary of the diocese of Dublin returns.[35]

This summary contains population figures for the unions of Bray and Delgany and for the parishes of Newcastle and Powerscourt.[36] The accuracy of the figures is, of course, open to question and one would have to be wary about the personal agendas of the participating ministers. Certainly the accurate enumeration of a parish depended to a great extent on the commitment of the local clergyman to the making of a valid return and to him having an intimate knowledge of the parish.[37]

Terence O'Donnell has assumed that in the case of the Raphoe returns 'more likely the figures for Protestant families, that is families belonging to the Established Church, are correct. On the other hand the returns for Catholic families may be based simply on a rough calculation; but even so, they are probably not too far wide of the mark'.[38] Even if we assume that O'Donnell's hypothesis (that the Protestant returns are reasonably accurate) holds for the north-east Wicklow area, it is still certain that some people in each of the parishes under study will not have been enumerated. However, it has been shown that north-east Wicklow had a substantial Protestant population from at least as early as the 1660s and the individual local clergyman would, therefore, have had a good knowledge of a larger proportion of the local population than would a minister in areas with few Protestants. Thus, if it is presumed that the ministers in the north-east Wicklow parishes did not wish to deliberately falsify the returns for their parish then it is probable that the Protestant returns for the area were reasonably accurate.[39]

It does seem likely that the estimate for the number of Protestants in each parish was more accurate than the estimate for Catholics for two obvious reasons. Firstly, the Penal Laws were still on the statute books, although they were honoured more in the breach than in the observance by the 1760s. Perhaps, therefore, Catholics remained somewhat reluctant to openly express their religion. Also, through no fault of his own, the Protestant clergymen would have had a greater familiarity with their own flock than with the papist communities. How could it be otherwise? If we assume, therefore, an omission rate of 5 per cent for Protestants and 10 per cent for Roman Catholics,[40] adjusted Census figures for north-east Wicklow and south-east Dublin may be calculated. These adjusted figures are shown in table 4.

Table 4 Adjusted figures for the Religious Census of 1766 for parishes in north-east Wicklow and south-east Dublin

Parish	Persons		Adjusted figures		% Prot.
	Prot.	Papist	Prot.	Papist	
Bray, Connagh &					
Kiltiernan	332 est.	1,178 est.	349	1,296	21.20
Powerscourt	360 est.	1,433 est.	378	1,576	19.34
Delgany union					
Delgany	315	545	331	600	35.55
Kilcoole	190	874	200	961	17.18
Killmaccnoge	78	577	82	635	11.43
Total for Delgany union	583	1,996	613	2,196	21.80
Newcastle	370	1,460	389	1,606	19.48

(Source: Summary Vol. Dublin Diocese (N.A.I. M 2476 (i)))

These Religious Census figures are the earliest genuine parish census and religious breakdown figures that are available for north-east Wicklow and they allow a critical eye to be cast on the population estimates based on hearth-tax figures that were presented in table 2. The hearth-money rolls suggested that the proportion of Protestants in the various parishes under study ranged from over 30 per cent in Delgany to over 55 per cent in Bray. The 1766 figures (ranging from below 12 per cent in Kilmacanoge to 36 per cent in Delgany) seem more realistic as they are more in line with the figures that were reported by the nineteenth-century censuses (table 13). Delgany, the least Protestant of the parishes under study in the 1660s (table 2), emerges as the most Protestant parish by 1766, a fact that was confirmed by the 1831 census.

The Religious Census also shows the population to have grown in the century between 1669 and 1766. As was seen in table 2, the population of the Delgany union in 1669 was estimated to be in the region of 1,450 and there were over 1,000 people living in Newcastle parish. By 1766, the population of both of these geographic areas had doubled, to 2,800 in the Delgany parishes and 2,000 in Newcastle. This modest population growth is supported by the analysis of the Delgany parish records outlined in the next chapter. As will be seen, population growth between 1669 and 1766 was not uniform and in particular, the 1740s and 1750s were difficult decades during which the population contracted.

Kilcoole appears to have been the most densely populated parish in north-east Wicklow in 1766 (table 5), as was the case in 1669. Delgany parish, by contrast, had been thinly populated in 1669 but had become the second most densely populated parish in the area by 1766.[41] Kilmacanoge, the third parish in the Delgany union experienced more modest population growth between 1669 and 1766 and was relatively thinly populated in 1766 in comparison with its neighbours.

Table 5 Estimated population density in north-east Wicklow parishes in 1766 (Area (acres) from *Census of Ireland 1861 – General report*, pp 120–2)

Parish	Area (acres)	Estimated population	No. of acres per person in 1766	Rank
Kilcoole	4,476	1,126	3.98	1
Delgany	3,978	909	4.38	2
Newcastle	11,776	1,937	6.08	3
Kilmacanoge	5,401	694	7.78	4
Powerscourt	18,938	1,897	9.98	5
Bray	2,986	N/A	N/A	N/A

Unfortunately there are no detailed census or census substitute figures available for the area between 1669 and 1766. However, there does exist a hearth roll summary for the county which was copied from the hearth-tax returns in the Public Record Office shortly before the destruction of the Four Courts.[42] This summary only lists hearth and house aggregates for most Wicklow parishes for 1739 and hearth aggregates for some parishes for 1748[43] and its importance derives from the dearth of other population level sources for the area for the years between 1669 and 1766. The data in this summary for the parishes studied in this chapter are shown in table 6.

Table 6 Hearth-roll summary for 1739 and 1748 for the parishes of north-east Wicklow (Source, N.L.I., Ms 7227)

Parish (listed)	Parish (modern spelling)	Barony	1739 Houses	Hearths	1748 Hearths
Up. Ncastle	Newcastle Upper	Newcastle	202	254	250
Lr. Ncastle	Newcastle Lower	Newcastle	116	183	186
Killcool	Kilcoole	Newcastle	175	248	255
Dellgany	Delgany	Half Rathdown	119	176	180
Kilmacanoge	Kilmacanoge	Half Rathdown	183	227	199
Poorscourt	Powerscourt	Half Rathdown	221	303	285
Bray	Bray	Half Rathdown	100	162	174

There is no indication of either population levels or religious breakdown in this hearth roll summary. However, by using a multiplier as before, a fair population estimate for 1739 can be determined. Furthermore, as the ratio of hearths to houses is known for 1739, if it is assumed that the same ratio held in 1748 then the number of houses in each parish in that year can be approximated and population estimates derived. Earlier the average number of people per house was estimated at 5.5 for the 1660s and if this figure is again used the resulting parish population estimates for 1739 and 1748 are shown in table 7.

Dickson *et al* have stated that 'the hearth-tax returns for the first half of the [eighteenth] century are relatively 'good' [but] that there is a perceptible

Table 7 Population estimates for parishes of north-east Wicklow in 1739 and 1748

Parish (modern spelling)	Houses (1739)	Population multiplier (5.5)	1739 ratio, hearths: houses	Estimate of no. of houses in 1748	Population (1748) multiplier (5.5)
Newcastle Upr.	202	1,111	1.26	199	1,095
Newcastle Lr.	116	638	1.58	118	649
Kilcoole	175	963	1.41	180	990
Delgany	119	655	1.48	122	671
Kilmacanoge	183	1,007	1.24	160	880
Powerscourt	221	1,216	1.37	208	1,144
Bray	100	550	1.62	107	589
Total	1,116	6,140		1,094	6,018

decline in their quality after mid-century'[44] and so these hearth and house figures can be assumed to be reasonably accurate. This does not mean, of course, that population estimates based on the hearth figures is accurate. For instance, it is assumed that the ratio of hearths to houses was consistent between 1739 and 1748. However if a large house was either constructed or destroyed between these dates then the hearths to houses ratio would have changed, which would result in a calculated population increase or fall by the method used here. In defence of this hearth-money summary, it will be seen in the next chapter that the population of the Delgany area declined in the 1740s and 1750s, before increasing again in the 1760s and the population estimates shown in table 7 do suggest a marginal population decline between 1739 and 1748. Furthermore, as the population declined in the 1740s and 1750s it is probable that the average number of people per house consequently fell during this period. For the purposes of this calculation we have assumed that the average number of people per house remained constant at 5.5. If this average did indeed fall between 1739 and 1748, however, then the population reduction would have been greater than that shown in table 7.

Statutory censuses were introduced in Ireland in 1813 and were held every ten years from 1821.[45] It was not until 1861, however, that an attempt was made through the census to enumerate the number of people subscribing to the various religious denominations in Ireland although in the 1830s a royal commission had been established to investigate 'the state of religious and other instruction in Ireland'.[46] As part of its remit the commission reported population and religious persuasion estimates on a parish basis for the whole country for 1831 and 1834. As it was considered too expensive to host a census-type enumeration, the 1831 census returns were used as the basis for the enumeration. The returns were referred back to the original enumerators, or other suitably qualified people, for them to fill in the religious denomination of those enumerated three years earlier.[47] The commissioners also made estimates of the population and religious breakdown for each parish for 1834.[48] To reduce any suspicion of bias, the parish statistics were presented to the ministers of religion of the various denominations, inviting them to comment on their accuracy or otherwise and in many cases the local minister or priest provided the parish statistics.[49] By including Roman Catholic priests in the enumeration process, one source of error in the 1766 Religious Census was automatically removed.

The nineteenth century was a time of questioning and discovery and the government launched numerous inquiries into all aspects of daily life throughout the United Kingdom. Societies such as the Dublin Society[50] and the Farming Society[51] also initiated agricultural inquiries and county surveys commencing in the early years of that century. With this new interest in surveys, statistical analysis became more professional than it had been previously and we can consequently have greater confidence in the figures produced in the nineteenth century than with earlier figures. This is not to argue that they are without their faults and inaccuracies. Lee has criticised the pre-Famine censuses as being both inconsistent and inaccurate[52] and doubtless he would equally criticise the figures presented in the education commissioner's report. However, one can strongly argue that the population and religious breakdown figures for 1831 and 1834 are likely to be more accurate than were those produced by the Religious Census seventy years previously. The census and education report figures for south-east Dublin and north-east Wicklow are shown in table 8.

Table 8 Population and religious breakdown figures from the *First report of commissioners of public instruction*, 1835, H.C. 1835 [45], xxxiii, pp 96b–124b)

Parish	Prot.	Roman Cath.	Presbyterian	Other Prot.	Total	% Prot.
1831 census						
Bray	874	2,629	6		3,509	24.91
Delgany	1,032	1,236			2,268	45.50
Kilcoole	739	1,620			2,359	31.33
Kilmacanoge	192	944			1,136	16.90
Delgany, Kilcoole and Kilmacanoge	1,963	3,800			5,763	34.06
Powerscourt	1,608	2,752	4	4	4,368	36.81
Newcastle Upr. + Lr.	984	2,886			3,870	25.43
Kiltiernan	155	758			913	16.98
Oldconnaught	560	1,380		7	1,947	28.76
1834 estimate						
Bray	603	2,570	22		3,195	18.87
Delgany, Kilcoole and Kilmacanoge	1,725	3,931			5,656	30.50
Powerscourt	1,656	2,834	4	4	4,498	36.84
Newcastle Upr. + Lr.	851	2,973			3,824	22.24
Kiltiernan	155	759			914	16.96
Oldconnaught	581	1,400			1,981	29.33

The proportion of Protestants in the various parishes in the 1830s is reasonably similar to the proportions reported by the 1766 Religious Census. Delgany parish again emerges as the most Protestant parish (45 per cent in 1831) whereas Kilmacanoge and Kiltiernan are the least Protestant with less than 17 per cent of the population recorded as Protestants. Also, the popular impression of the Irish population growing rapidly in the latter part of the eighteenth and early part of the nineteenth century is supported by these figures. Between

1766 (Religious Census) and 1831 the population of the Delgany union
advanced rapidly from 2,700 to 5,750. This increase of more than 110 per cent
occurred in a little over six decades whereas in the century prior to the
Religious Census the population had only doubled. Newcastle parish
experienced a similar demographic trend with the population doubling to
about 1,900 in the century before 1766 and doubling again to about 3,870
between 1766 and 1831.

Parish population density figures for 1831 are shown in table 9. Kilcoole
parish grew more slowly than either Bray or Delgany (table 5 for 1766 figures)
between 1766 and 1831 and Delgany parish had become more densely
populated than its southern neighbour by the 1830s. The population density
of Kilmacanoge relative to its immediate neighbours had continued to fall and
by 1831 it had become the least densely populated parish in the area.

Table 9 Estimated population density in north-east Wicklow parishes in
1831 (Area (acres) from *Census of Ireland 1861 – General report*, pp 120–2)

Parish	Area (acres)	Estimated population	No. of acres per person in 1831	Rank
Bray	2,986	3,509	0.85	1
Delgany	3,978	2,268	1.75	2
Kilcoole	4,476	2,359	1.90	3
Newcastle	11,776	3,870	3.04	4
Powerscourt	18,938	4,368	4.34	5
Kilmacanoge	5,401	1,136	4.75	6

In general, the number of Protestants in the area increased relative to non-
Protestants between the Religious Census and the 1830s. The Protestant
proportion of the population increased from 36 per cent to 45 per cent in
Delgany, from 18 per cent to 31 per cent in Kilcoole and from 12 per cent to
17 per cent in Kilmacanoge. As would be expected, the estimated religious
breakdown figures for 1834 are very similar to those of 1831 with the
exception of Bray parish and the union of Delgany (see table 10), both of
which exhibited sharp drops in Protestant numbers. The remarkable drop in
the total population in Bray and in the Protestant population in both Bray and
the Delgany union between 1831 and 1834 is clearly outlined in table 10. In
Bray the population contracted by almost 10 per cent but the Protestant
population fell more dramatically from almost a quarter of the total population
to less than one in five while in Delgany the Protestant population shrank by
over 12 per cent. Oldconnaught, by contrast, experienced a population
increase between these years.

Table 10 Proportionate change in both Protestant population and total population between 1831 and 1834 for Bray, Oldconnaught and the Delgany union.

Parish	1831 % Prot.	1834 % Prot.	Change in	
			Protestant population	Total population
Bray	24.95	19.00	−31.01%	−9.42%
Oldconnaught	28.87	29.33	3.75%	2.11%
Delgany union	34.06	30.50	−12.12%	−1.86%

The commissioners explained the decline in Protestant numbers in Bray in the following fashion; 'the census of 1831 was taken in the summer when there were many lodgers in the town for the purpose of sea bathing; that of 1834 in winter, which may account for the decrease'.[53] As a similar comment was made for Newcastle,[54] it seems reasonable that the population of Delgany and Kilcoole, located between these two parishes, may also have been artificially exaggerated in 1831. Well-to-do Protestants accounted for a large portion of the tourist traffic at this time and the commissioners did presume in the case of Newcastle that 'there is probably not the same fluctuation in the Roman Catholic population'.[55]

As was mentioned earlier, the 1861 census was the first census to officially inquire into the religious persuasion of Irish people and this information was reported on a parish basis. The relevant population and religion figures for the parishes under study are shown in table 11. Lee's comment on the accuracy of pre-Famine censuses[56] is undoubtedly no less applicable to this census than it is to the censuses to which it referred. However, the figures are likely to be at least as accurate as the 1831 and 1834 returns and are certainly more accurate than the various seventeenth and eighteenth century figures that have already been considered.

The religious breakdown figures in the 1861 census are quite similar to the figures for religious practice in the 1830s shown in table 8. Delgany parish was still the most Protestant of the parishes under study with almost 40 per cent of the population proclaiming to be members of the Church of Ireland. The new and fast-growing town of Greystones was overwhelmingly Protestant at this stage. In relative terms, Kilmacanoge's Protestant population had increased from 17 per cent of the parish in 1831 to 23 per cent while Kilcoole's Protestant population had contracted to 21 per cent of the total population in the same period.

In absolute terms, the parishes of Kilmacanoge and Oldconnaught are unique in that the population of these parishes actually increased significantly between 1831 and 1861. The population of Kilmacanoge increased by 27 per

Table 11   1861 census figures and population breakdown for north-east
Wicklow and south-east Dublin

Region/town	Total pop.	C. of I. – Male	C. of I. – Female	C. of I. – Total	Proportion C. of I.
Newcastle Lower	743	126	156	282	37.95%
Newcastle Upper (rural part)	1,186	66	93	159	13.41%
Newtown Mount Kennedy	566	26	45	71	12.54%
Total – Newcastle parish	**2,495**	**218**	**294**	**512**	**20.52%**
Kilcoole (rural part)	1,116	134	135	269	24.10%
Kilcoole town	418	26	19	45	10.77%
Kilpedder town	195	25	18	43	22.05%
Total – Kilcoole parish	**1,729**	**185**	**172**	**357**	**20.65%**
Kilmacanoge parish	**1,446**	**150**	**187**	**337**	**23.31%**
Bray (rural part)	700	47	61	108	15.43%
Bray town	2,736	204	284	488	17.84%
Newtown Vevay town	232	7	17	24	10.34%
Total – Bray parish	**3,668**	**258**	**362**	**620**	**16.90%**
Powerscourt (rural part)	1,904	223	224	447	23.48%
Enniskerry town	374	67	83	150	40.11%
Total – Powerscourt par.	**2,278**	**290**	**307**	**597**	**26.21%**
Delgany (rural part)	1,205	223	207	430	35.68%
Delgany town	248	47	64	111	44.76%
Greystones town	238	93	75	168	70.59%
Grundy's Row town	139	10	8	18	12.95%
Killincarrig town	119	16	31	47	39.50%
Total – Delgany parish	**1,949**	**389**	**385**	**774**	**39.71%**
Kiltiernan parish	**775**			**98**	**12.65%**
Oldconnaught (rural part)	1,227			356	29.01%
Little Bray town	1,446			177	12.24%
Total – Oldconnaught parish	**2,673**			**533**	**19.94%**

(Source, Wicklow figures from *Census of Ireland 1861, pt. v*, pp 120–123. Dublin figures
from *Census of Ireland 1861, pt. iv*, pp 44–45)

cent, from 1,136 in 1831 to 1,446 in 1861 while Oldconnaught's population expanded by a remarkable 37 per cent, from 1,947 to 2,673. During this period the population of all other parishes in the area, with the sole exception of Bray, was contracting in the aftermath of the Famine. The population of the Delgany union fell by over 600 (11 per cent) to about 5,100 between 1831 and 1861 while the population of Newcastle parish fell by 1,400 to almost 2,500, a drop of over 35 per cent.

Parish population density figures for 1861 are shown in table 12. By 1861 Bray had a substantially greater population density than any of the surrounding Wicklow parishes. Delgany parish had the greatest density of population of the three Delgany union parishes and Kilcoole was also densely populated. Kilmacanoge parish, by contrast, was relatively thinly populated, as had it been in 1831.

Table 12 Estimated population density in north-east Wicklow parishes in 1861 (Area (acres) from *Census of Ireland 1861 – General report*, pp 120–2)

Parish	Area (acres)	Estimated population	No. of acres per person in 1861	Rank
Bray	2,986	3,668	0.81	1
Delgany	3,978	1,949	2.04	2
Kilcoole	4,476	1,729	2.59	3
Kilmacanoge	5,401	1,446	3.74	4
Newcastle	11,776	2,495	4.72	5
Powerscourt	18,938	2,278	8.31	6

In this chapter many of the various population and religious distribution sources available for a number of contiguous parishes in north-east Wicklow and south-east Dublin between the mid-seventeenth and the mid-nineteenth centuries have been analysed. It is clear from the available sources that the further back in time one goes the less reliable the figures become. For some of the earlier sources, namely the 1664 Dublin hearth-money roll, the 1669 Wicklow hearth money roll and the 1766 Religious Census figures, the reported figures have been modified to try to lessen the impact of suspected under-reporting. All of the various parish population and religious distribution figures considered in this chapter are summarised in table 13.[57]

Of all of the sources considered in this chapter, the greatest concern lies with the various seventeenth-century figures. Whereas the 1766 census seems to accurately determine the proportion of Protestants in the various north-east Wicklow parishes, surname analysis of the hearth-money figures appears to exaggerate the relative strength of Protestantism. In defence of the hearth-

Table 13 Adjusted estimates of the number of Protestants and number of people in the parishes under study, 1659–1861

Year		Kiltiernan	Old-connaught	Bray	Bray, Old-connaught and Kiltiernan	Powerscourt	Delgany	Kilcoole	Kilmacanoge	Delgany, Kilcoole and Kilmacanoge	Newcast
1630	Protestants	0	14	16	30	200	4	2	4	10	2
1659	Protestants	6	63								
	Population	42	309								
	% Protestant	14.29	20.39								
1664	Protestants	40	119								
	Population	113	356								
	% Protestant	35.11	33.33								
1669	Protestants			145		320	95	258	188	540	41
	Population			258		709	308	677	489	1,474	102
	% Protestant			56.19		45.18	30.74	38.05	38.46	36.54	40.2
1739	Population			550		1,216	655	963	1,007	2,624	1,74
1748	Population			591		1,143	669	990	882	2,541	1,74
1766	Protestants				349	378	331	200	82	613	38
	Population				1,645	1,954	931	1,161	717	2,809	1,99
	% Protestant				21.20	19.34	35.55	17.18	11.43	19.48	
1831	Protestants	155	560	874	1,589	1,608	1,032	739	192	1,963	98
	Population	913	1,947	3,509	6,369	4,368	2,268	2,359	1,136	5,763	3,87
	% Protestant	16.98	28.76	24.91	24.95	36.81	45.50	31.33	16.90	34.06	25.4
1834	Protestants	155	581	603	1,339	1,656				1,725	85
	Population	914	1,981	3,195	6,090	4,498				5,656	3,82
	% Protestant	16.96	29.33	18.87	21.99	36.82				30.50	22.2
1861	Protestants	98	533	620	1,251	597	774	357	337	1,468	51
	Population	775	2,673	3,668	7,116	2,278	1,949	1,729	1,446	5,124	2,49
	% Protestant	12.65	19.94	16.90	17.58	26.21	39.71	20.65	23.31%	28.65	20.5

money rolls, it can be said that the demographic make up of the area and the religious balance in particular could have changed substantially in the 100 years between the compiling of the Dublin and Wicklow hearth-money rolls in the 1660s and the 1766 Religious Census. It must be remembered, too, that a land settlement had been effected in the aftermath of the Restoration and this may have had a short-term impact on the tenancy situation in the 1660s. Also, despite the various sources used in the construction of this demographic portrait (an ecclesiastical enquiry, a hearth-tax roll and hearth roll summaries, census figures and an education report) it is comforting to observe that the ratio of the enumerated population between parishes remains fairly consistent between 1666 and 1831. For instance, we have seen that Bray was the least populated parish in north-east Wicklow in 1669. Both of the hearth-roll summaries of the mid-eighteenth century also found Bray to be the smallest parish, as did the 1766 Religious Census. It was not until Bray began to attract Dublin's *nouveau riche* in the nineteenth century that its relative population increased with respect to its neighbouring parishes.[58]

Figure 1 plots the ratio of the populations of Delgany, Kilmacanoge, Kilcoole, Powerscourt and Newcastle to the population of Bray for various

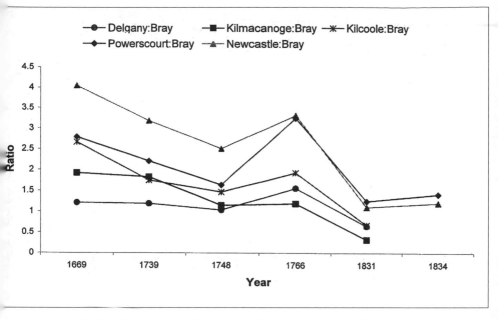

1. Ratios of population of various parishes in north-east Wicklow to
population of Bray, 1669–1834

years.[59] As can be seen, the relative size of the various parishes remained much
the same between 1669 and 1831, showing that while the hearth-money
figures and the religious census data may not have been completely accurate,
nonetheless the reported figures were certainly in the right ballpark. Thus,
despite the many doubts one may have about the pre-nineteenth century
sources, they are of great importance in the construction of a demographic
portrait of north-east Wicklow and south-east Dublin.

The population and religious distribution findings for Delgany, Kilcoole
and Kilmacanoge parishes between 1669 and 1861 are shown in figure 2. It
was seen that the area was relatively thinly populated in the 1660s and that
Protestants comprised a significant proportion of the entire population at that
time. Furthermore, it was observed that Protestants tended to cluster in certain
townlands and many of the quasi-urban settlements were principally or
exclusively Protestant.

The 1669 hearth-money roll for Wicklow showed Delgany parish to be
thinly populated in the 1660s and it was the least Protestant of the eight
parishes studied. Within a century, however, the 1766 Religious Census
recorded that the population of Delgany parish had increased substantially and
also that the parish had become the most Protestant parish in the area.[60]
Furthermore, it was seen that the trend suggested by the 1766 census was

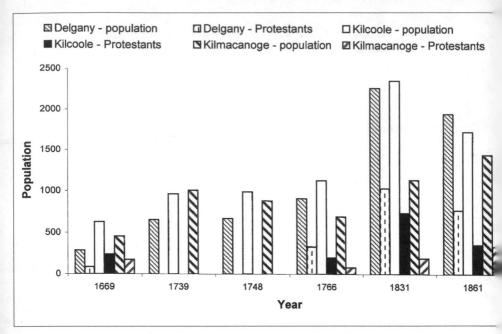

2. Total population and protestant population in Delgeny, Kilcoole and
Kilmacanoge parishes, 1669–1861

confirmed by nineteenth-century census figures. The 1831 census reported
that over 45 per cent of the parish was Protestant while the 1861 census
recorded a comparable figure of almost 40 per cent.

Kilcoole parish, immediately to the south of Delgany, had a markedly
different demographic experience from that of Delgany in the two centuries
following the Restoration. In 1669 Kilcoole had a high population in
comparison with neighbouring parishes and had a Protestant population as
high as 38 per cent. By 1766, however, the Religious Census reported that less
than 18 per cent of the inhabitants of the parish were Protestant. This means
that there was either substantial population movements within the parish in
the preceding century or else that either the hearth-money roll or the
Religious Census (or both) is inaccurate. The 1831 census again recorded a
substantial Protestant population in Kilcoole (31 per cent), declining to slightly
over 20 per cent by 1861. Furthermore, this census showed that in the
preceding two centuries the population of Kilcoole had grown relatively
slowly and that Delgany, Powerscourt, Newcastle, Bray and Oldconnaught had
larger populations than Kilcoole.

Kilmacanoge parish had a higher proportion of Protestants (38.5 per cent)
than either Kilcoole or Delgany in 1669 and had a larger population than

Delgany. As with Kilcoole, however, the 1669 figures for Kilmacanoge contrast sharply with the figures recorded in the Religious Census. Furthermore, by 1766 Kilmacanoge's population had increased by just 50 per cent during the preceding century and it had the lowest population of the parishes studied. In comparison the population of Kilcoole parish advanced by almost 80 per cent and the population of Delgany by more than 200 per cent in the same period. By 1861 Delgany's population had increased by nearly 600 per cent since the 1660s whereas Kilmacanoge and Kilcoole had experienced more modest population growth.

From the cradle to the grave:
Natural population change in the
Delgany union, 1666–1779

In the previous chapter the general population trends in north-east Wicklow and south-east Dublin in the two hundred years following the Restoration were outlined. In this chapter these trends will be verified primarily through an examination of the Delgany union parish records. In general, it must be said that Irish historians, unlike their British colleagues, have tended to shy away from using parish records as a demographic source and demographic studies in this country are consequently at a far less advanced stage.[1] The primary reason for this reluctance to delve wholeheartedly into parish-registers studies is that the earliest registers are predominantly Protestant and therefore often unrepresentative of the majority population in a locality. However, as north-east Wicklow has had a significant Protestant minority since at least the 1660s, the Delgany Church of Ireland registers are an important demographic source for the region.

Some of the more important Irish demographic investigation has focussed on Ulster where the Protestant population has been historically strong. Valerie Morgan used Church of Ireland parish registers to study the population histories of Blaris (Lisburn), Coleraine and Magherafelt while William Macafee made extensive use of Protestant registers in his study of the Maghera region in the seventeenth and eighteenth centuries.[2] Roman Catholic records, by contrast, have been less widely used for early demographic study because recording of these registers generally commenced more recently than did the comparable Protestant records. Relatively few Roman Catholic records commence before the nineteenth century whereas Protestant parishes were instructed to record baptisms and burials from as early as 1634.[3] Despite this instruction Petty commented in 1672 that 'Registers of Burials, Births and Marriages, are not yet kept in *Ireland*, though of late begun in *Dublin*, but imperfectly'.[4]

In the half-barony of Rathdown in Wicklow, for example, mid-seventeenth century Protestant church records are available for the Bray union[5] (from 1666), Powerscourt parish[6] (from 1662) and the Delgany union[7] (from 1666) whereas Roman Catholic records do not commence until 1792 for Bray parish[8] and as late as 1825 for Enniskerry parish.[9] Of the twenty-one Roman

Catholic parishes in County Wicklow, the earliest Roman Catholic records are for Wicklow parish (from 1747) and only seven Catholic parishes have records that commence before the nineteenth century.[10]

It is an accepted fact that all historical records are biased and parish records are no less prone to biases than are other sources. An obvious bias in parochial records is that by their nature they are incomplete. No matter how well kept the records appear to be, it is inevitable that entries have been, either by accident or by design, omitted from them. Deliberate omissions from the records may have arisen from parish or vestry policy with regard to certain categories of entries. When studying baptismal records, for instance, one must consider whether the parish had any policy on recording stillborn births, children who died before baptism, children who were not baptised, children who lived in the parish but were baptised in another parish, children who were born out of wedlock or children whose parents could not afford to pay the baptismal fees. Comparable questions can also be applied to the burial and marriage registers.

Accidental omissions from the registers may have occurred if a new church minister proved to be less committed to the accurate recording of baptisms, marriages and burials in the parish. One can often observe a change in the quality of the record-keeping when an incumbent was replaced. Furthermore, war, famine or other catastrophes may have disrupted the accurate recording of entries or at the very least made accurate recording more difficult. Indecipherable entries and torn or missing pages also effectively reduce the completeness of the church records.

A second important bias in the Protestant church records concerns the fact that, outside of Ulster and parts of the east coast south of Dublin, Protestantism was a minority religion with a membership that often comprised the social and economic elite. It is quite a challenge, therefore, to make general assumptions about the population trends of an entire people from the baptismal, marriage and burial records of a small minority. Protestant church records are obviously best suited to demographic study of an area that had a high proportion of Protestants. In such areas, it was more likely that Protestants populated the entire social spectrum rather than just the upper echelons of society.[11] If Protestants were as likely to be labourers as landowners, then, as a group, they were less insulated from the recurring challenges of famine, shortage and diseases.

The Local Population Studies group in England has outlined six tests that can be applied to parish registers to determine both their completeness and their suitability as sources for demographic research.[12] While these tests may be more applicable to English parish registers they raise a number of interesting questions that may be asked of Irish records. One of the tests, concerning the extent of nonconformity in the parish, is particularly interesting in the case of Ireland. As religious activity on the part of nonconformists was curtailed by law in the seventeenth and eighteenth centuries Protestant records can often be found to contain entries for non-Protestants.[13] The burial records are particularly prone to containing non-Protestant entries because parish cemeteries were owned by the Church of Ireland and were often the only burial place in the locality.[14] In contrast, baptismal record entries are generally exclusively Anglican[15] while marriage records can list non-Anglicans in the case of mixed marriage couples.

It is suggested that if the average number of entries per annum for the parish records does not exceed 100 then the records should not be used.[16] This is one area where the rules for England and Ireland must diverge. As the relative strength of Protestants in Ireland was much lower than in England, there were consequently fewer baptisms, marriages and burials recorded in Irish parishes per annum. Nonconformists in England were a small minority in comparison to Ireland, where the vast majority of the population had rejected the Protestant church. The comfort of working with large numbers of entries per annum is, therefore, often not available to Irish demographic historians. Whilst the reason behind the 100-entry lower limit is obvious, in that it is relatively easy to spot short gaps if no entries were recorded for a month or more, it will be seen that sophisticated statistical analysis can still be performed on a smaller sample.

As has been noted, baptism, marriage and burial records commence in the 1660s for the unions of Bray and Delgany and for Powerscourt parish. However, in comparison with the Powerscourt and Bray registers the Delgany records are significantly more complete and more reliable as the Powerscourt and Bray registers were poorly kept for the seventeenth and first half of the eighteenth centuries and lengthy gaps frequently occur in the Powerscourt records, in particular. The Bray registers also display features that suggest that they are likely not to be the originals but casually transcribed copies.[17] In places the records are incorrectly sequenced and family sequences can occasionally be observed, an example of which is shown below where these five entries are listed one after the other in the baptism registers.

Richard son to William and Dorothy Strong 11 August 1728

Susana dr to William and Dorothy Strong 7 April 1731

William son to William and Dorothy Strong, 21 Sept. 1738

Thomas son to William and Dorothy Strong, 3 Nov. 1741

William son to John and Catherine Thorp, born 28 April and baptised 5 May 1740.

The Delgany records, on the other hand are generally legible and there are relatively few incidents where names have either been added in the margins or where entries were added retrospectively thus affecting the chronological order of the records. They are also more complete than either the earliest Bray or Powerscourt records are.[18]

What makes the Delgany records particularly valuable as an historical source is that most of the earliest entries (1666–*c.* 1730) are quite detailed, containing the father and mother's name of baptised or buried children and also the townland in which the family lived. The townland information is especially important because it allows one to differentiate between families with the same surname. By contrast, the Bray and Powerscourt entries for the seventeenth and eighteenth century are less detailed and rarely contain this crucial townland information.

The first book of the Delgany registers records baptisms, marriages and burials in the Delgany union between 1666 and 1779. As this time period coincides with the period of modest population growth in Ireland before the population trend assumed its tragic upward spiral in the decades before the Famine, it represents an ideal unit of study.

Deciding on the spatial extent of a study based on the first book of the registers, however, is a little more difficult. It was mentioned earlier that Newcastle parish was closely linked to the Delgany union and entries for Newcastle are included in the Delgany register up until 1698. The removal of Newcastle entries from the Delgany registers meant that the number of incidents of baptisms and burials fell in comparison with the preceding years. The average number of baptisms recorded in the five year period, 1693–7 was 23.8. With Newcastle parish records not being recorded beyond 1698, the average baptisms dropped to eighteen for the five years, 1698–1702 and 16.8 for the five years, 1703–7. The average number of baptisms for successive five-year periods remained less than the 1693–7 average until an average of twenty five baptisms were recorded for the half-decade, 1763–7. A similar, but less obvious pattern is exhibited in the burial records. Because Newcastle entries are only recorded in the registers between 1666 and 1698, it is logical to exclude Newcastle from the scope of this study. This is relatively easily accomplished because as was already noted most of the early records contain townland information. It is thus a matter of examining all entries prior to 1698 to see if they relate to Newcastle residents and excluding them if they are.

Kilmacanoge parish, however, also presents difficulties. The northern and western parts of Kilmacanoge were nearer to the churches at Bray and Powerscourt than to Delgany church and it is highly likely that a proportion of parishioners in these areas must have practised their religion in the neighbouring parish. Although the extent of Kilmacanoge residents attending other churches is unknown, it seems reasonable to assume that most Protestants in the northern and western parts of Kilmacanoge would have gravitated towards the nearby churches of Powerscourt and Bray to be baptised, married or buried.

In the first chapter the proportion of Protestants in Kilmacanoge was estimated at over 38 per cent in 1669. However, it has been shown that the

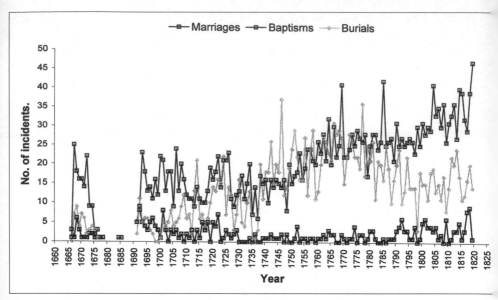

3. Baptisms, marriages and burials in the parishes of Delgany, Kilcoole and
Kilmacanoge (1666–1819)

northern and western parts of the parish had higher proportions of Protestants
and Protestants may indeed have outnumbered Catholics in the four
townlands of Kilcroney, Fassaroe, Ballyorney and Coolakay.[19] Because there is
uncertainty concerning the religious practice of Kilmacanoge's Protestants it
would be wise to also exclude the parish from this study. Unfortunately,
however, it is a far more difficult task to exclude Kilmacanoge from the study
than it is to exclude Newcastle because as the practice of recording townland
information ceased in the early 1730s it is virtually impossible to identify
entries for Kilmacanoge residents after 1731. Thus, although we would wish
to exclude Kilmacanoge from the study it is impractical to do so.

The remainder of this chapter will, therefore, focus on using the first book
of the Delgany registers to analyse population change in the parishes of
Delgany, Kilcoole and parts of Kilmacanoge between 1666 and 1760. Figure 3
shows the baptisms, marriages and burials, excluding Newcastle inhabitants,
per month as recorded in Delgany parish records between 1666 and 1819. An
obvious feature of the graph is the gap in recordings that commenced in the
1670s and ceased in 1691. It will be seen that this hiatus presents us with
numerous difficulties when analysing the records.

The varying trends in baptisms and burials between 1666 and 1819 is also
obvious in figure 3. A high number of baptisms were recorded in the 1660s
and, with the resumption of recording in the 1690s, baptisms remained at a
high level until 1705. Between 1705 and 1735 the level of recorded baptisms

dropped substantially with the exception of the period, 1715–22. From 1735 the number of baptisms began to increase again, in particular during the years 1735–65, after which a levelling off occurred.

The burial records, by contrast, show a different pattern to that displayed by the baptism graph. Burials were low in the 1660s and remained so until 1735, albeit with some dramatic peaks in burials between 1710 and 1725. After 1735 the number of burials increased significantly and the burials per annum exceeded the number of baptisms for twelve of the sixteen years between 1740 and 1755. In the 1760s the number of burials began to reduce again and a substantial differential opened up between baptisms and burials. By 1795 baptisms were exceeding burials by an average of more than twelve per annum.

The most striking feature of figure 3, however, is the dramatic peaks which periodically occurred in both the level of baptisms and burials during the eighteenth century. In the first half of the century burial peaks (exceeding nineteen in a calendar year) occurred in 1714 (twenty-one), 1724 (twenty-two), 1738 (twenty), 1742 (twenty-six), 1744 (twenty) and 1746 (thirty-seven). After 1750 the trend in the number of burials increased significantly with large peaks (burials exceeding twenty-seven per year) occurring in 1751 (twenty-nine), 1758 (twenty-nine), 1763 (twenty-six), 1766–8 (thirty-one, twenty-eight and twenty-nine respectively), 1772 (twenty-eight) and 1777 (thirty-six). After 1777, however, the number of burials recorded does not exceed twenty-seven again until 1837. This change in the trend of burials is remarkable and will be analysed in detail later in this chapter.

Burials reached an all time peak for the 1666–1819 period in 1746 and peaked again in 1777. The extent of the difficulties experienced during these two years, however, is not immediately evident from these cold statistics. If one considers that in the two and a half centuries between 1666 and 1900, only 1837 (forty-two) and 1840 (forty-seven) had a higher number of recorded burials than during 1746 even though the population of the Delgany union had more than trippled in the century following the 1740s (table 13) one may begin to get some sense of the hardships that had to be endured during that tragic year.

Obvious peaks in baptisms occurred in 1667 (twenty-five), 1672 (twenty-two) and 1693 (twenty-three) and after 1700 baptism peaks (baptisms greater than twenty-five) occurred in 1760 (twenty-six) 1762 (twenty-eight), 1764 (thirty-two) 1766 (thirty), 1768 (twenty-five), 1769 (forty-one) and with increasing regularity after 1770. Very high numbers of baptisms occurred in 1769, 1785 (forty-two) and 1804 (forty-one) at a time when five-year averages were 26.8, 28.6 and 33.6 respectively.

Baptisms reached or exceeded forty per year in 1769, 1804 and 1814 and an all time high figure in 1785. In figure 4 known years of national distress during the period 1666–1819 have been superimposed over the baptism, marriage and burial graphs, allowing for the determination as to whether

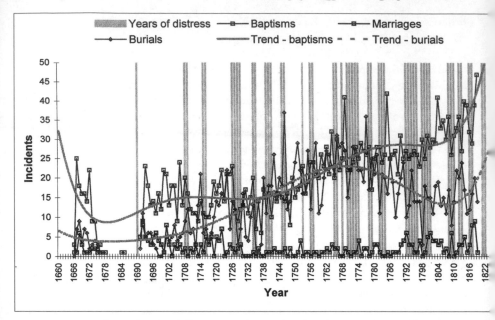

4. Years of national distress superimposed on baptism, marriage and burial
graphs for Delgany, Kilcoole and Kilmacanoge parishes.
Best-fit lines have been added for the baptism and burial graphs.

there was any link between general distress and the baptism or burial rate.[20]
Best-fit lines have also been added for the baptism and burial graphs and these
can be viewed as a crude average of the number of baptisms and burials
recorded during the period.

As can be seen, the four major peaks in the baptism rate in 1769, 1785, 1804
and 1814–15 occur immediately after known periods of distress. On a more
general level, it appears that incidents of baptisms tended to dip during
extended periods of distress. Instances of this can be seen in the case of the
1708–9 period (peak in wheat prices) where baptisms dropped from twenty
in 1708 to sixteen and twelve respectively in 1709 and 1710.[21] The four years
of poor grain harvests between 1726–9[22] witnessed an increase in the numbers
on the parish poor list while at the same time recorded baptisms fell from
twenty-three in 1726 to eleven, nine and twelve in the following three years.[23]
Baptisms also dropped from a peak of forty-one in 1769 to the low to mid-
twenties during the five years of potato and grain shortage commencing in
1770.[24] This apparent link between distress and a falling baptism rate closely
matches what David Dickson has found for eighteenth-century Catholic
parishes in north Leinster.[25]

It is more difficult to determine a link between known periods of distress and
the burial pattern because we are dealing with fewer instances of burials than

baptisms although a weak correlation is evident. The burial peak of 1742, for instance, followed *Bliain an Áir* and the most devastating famine of the eighteenth century. Interestingly no Delgany vestry minutes were recorded for 1742 which may suggest that no cess was levied on the parishoners that year. Later in that decade when burials peaked in 1746 there is little on record to indicate the scale of the crisis in the Delgany area but interestingly no vestry minutes were recorded this year either.[26] It was very rare indeed for vestry minutes not to be recorded and aside from the years 1742 and 1746, vestry minutes are missing for only two other years during the eighteenth century (1703 and 1707). That no vestry minutes exist for 1742 and 1746 does seem more than coincidental and suggests that these years were particularly difficult for the area.

In the 1760s burials also increased during the potato and grain failure in the middle of the decade. Burials averaged 17.8 per year between 1756 and 1760, rising to 23.4 per year between 1761 and 1765 and twenty-six per year between 1766 and 1770.

It does seem from figure 4 that the correlation between increased burials and periods of shortage tended to lessen as the century progressed. Dickson has suggested that one should expect to find a weakening of the link between shortage and mortality in the nineteenth century as alternative sources of income became available.[27] However, from the burial trends shown in figure 4 there is some evidence to suggest that this link may have been weakening in the Delgany region during the eighteenth century.

Population change in a region is influenced by various factors including births, deaths and migration. For the purpose of this study, the differential between births and deaths will be termed the 'natural' (fertility related) population increase and all other influences will be termed 'non-fertility' related population growth. Figure 4, therefore, shows that after 1710 the natural rate of Protestant population growth in the Delgany area was positive but falling. As has been noted, during the 1740–55 period burials regularly exceeded baptisms and the average number of baptisms was less than the number of burials from about 1742 until the 1760s. This does not necessarily mean that the number of Protestants in the region was falling because non-fertility related growth factors have not been accounted for. It is clear, however, that the indigenous Protestant community in the Delgany area was finding it increasingly difficult to replenish itself from early in the eighteenth century and was actually failing to do so for much of the 1740s and 1750s.

The negative natural population growth that commenced at the start of the 1740s continued at an increasing rate until the mid-1750s after which it began to reduce. By the late-1760s natural Protestant population growth had again become positive and the growth was increasing until the end of the eighteenth century as the number of burials per year fell from the high levels of the mid-decades of the century. The trend in natural population growth shown in figure 4 corresponds very closely to the demographic picture of the area that

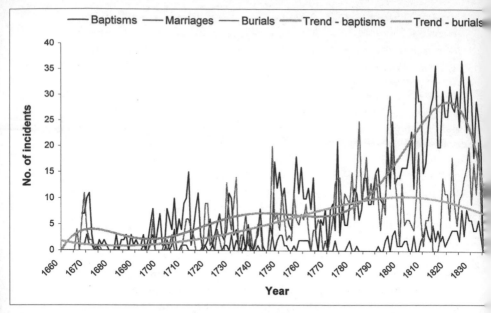

5. Trends in Baptism and burials in Bray parish, 1660–1840

was outlined in the first chapter. In particular, the negative natural population growth experienced during the 1740s and 1750s supports the suggestion made in the previous chapter that the population of the area fell between 1739 and 1748.

This curious trend in natural population growth will be examined in greater detail in the next chapter. There are, however, two possible explanations for the trend that spring immediately to mind. The first is that deaths may have increased and baptisms fallen in the 1740s as a result of a fall in living standards that must have been the practical result of that decade's shortages and distress. We have seen that the 1740s was a particularly difficult decade with the 1741 famine followed closely by the 1746 burial peak.

Although this idea of burials and baptisms being influenced by falling standards of living in the mid-eighteenth century is a convenient one, it can be easily refuted. It will be remembered that natural population growth in the area was actually falling over a fifty-year period, from the 1710s to the 1760s. It is unlikely that burials could be augmented and baptisms depressed over such a prolonged period. In addition, figure 4 suggests that food shortages were more common between 1770 and 1805 than between 1720 and 1770.

Also, it is implausible that serious distress could occur in the Delgany union between 1720 and 1760 and not in the neighbouring parishes of Powerscourt and Bray. Although the Bray and Powerscourt records are less complete than Delgany's, nonetheless trends in the natural rate of population growth during

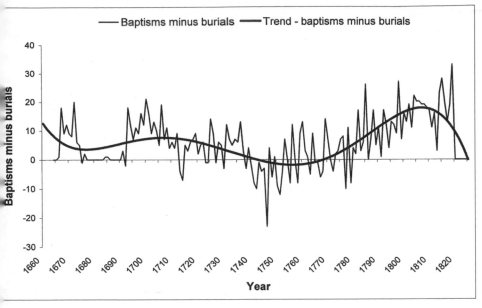

6. Baptisms minus burials in Delgany, Kilcoole and Kilmacanoge, 1666–1819, as recorded in the Delgany registers (trendline added).

the eighteenth century can still be determined for these parishes. The baptism and burial trends in Bray and Powerscourt are very similar and the Bray graph is shown for illustrative purposes in figure 5.[28] However, the Bray and Powerscourt trends contrast sharply with the Delgany trends shown in figure 4. Because of these differing trends in these coterminous areas then it seems unlikely that the Delgany natural population trend was influenced by prolonged distress.

The second possible explanation of the natural population growth trend centres around the likelihood that a 'greying' of the Protestant population may have occurred during the half-century centring on the year 1740. If children of tenants had to move out of the parish to obtain tenancies in neighbouring areas then as the population aged, the ratio of burials to baptisms would have increased. As will be seen in the next chapter, surname analysis of the parish records strongly supports this hypothesis. It will also be seen that immigration of young couples may have commenced in the 1760s, thus reducing the average age of the population. A falling age profile would tie in with the increase in baptisms and the reduction in burials that occurred in the 1760s.

A more revealing picture of natural population change is shown by figure 6, which plots the annual number of baptisms minus burials between 1666 and 1819. Years of distress, when burials exceeded baptisms, are readily evident in this graph. Clearly 1746 stands out as having been a uniquely difficult year.

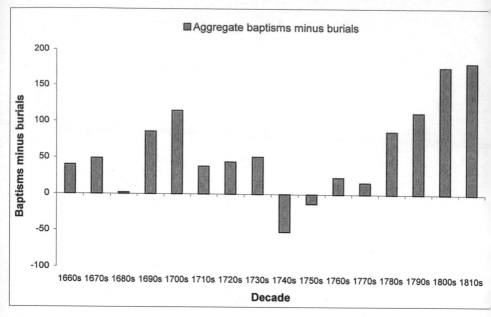

7. Aggregate baptisms minus burials on a decade-by-decade basis in Delgany,
Kilcoole and Kilmacanoge parishes between 1666–1819.

Furthermore, burials exceeded baptisms in eighteen of the thirty years
between 1740 and 1769. By contrast, in the century and a half between 1666
and 1819, burials exceeded baptisms for only thirty years.

The idea that the 1740s and 1750s were particularly difficult decades in
north-east Wicklow is reinforced by an aggregation of baptisms minus burials
on a decade-by-decade basis as is shown in figure 7. The 1690s and 1700s
appear to have been good years for the parish when the natural population
trend was positive and increasing. In the 1710s, 1720s and 1730s the natural
population increase was significantly lower possibly as a result of the periodic
food shortages shown in figure 4. The 1740s was clearly a particularly bad
decade in the area with burials outstripping baptisms by more than fifty.
Although 1746 was the worst year with twenty-three more burials than
baptisms recorded, all but two years in that decade (1747 and 1749)
experienced more burials than baptisms.

The number of burials remained greater than baptisms in the 1750s but by
the 1760s the natural population change had reverted to a positive, but small,
figure. The 1770s also appears to have been a troubled decade before a
significant population expansion commenced in the 1780s which continued
until the 1850s.

The Bray and Powerscourt figures are too unreliable to perform a similar
exercise on. Significantly, however, Bray did experience a peak in burials in

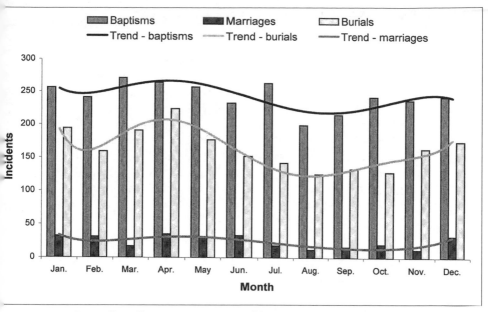

8. Seasonality of baptisms, marriages and burials in Delgany, Kilcoole and Kilmacanoge, 1666–1819

1747, the year after the burial peak in Delgany. Furthermore, of the twenty burials recorded in Bray in 1747, ten occurred in the first three months of the year. In Delgany in 1746, twenty of the thirty-seven burials recorded occurred in the last six months of the year. Thus, the 1746 Delgany burial peak and 1747 Bray peak may both be manifestations of an increased death rate with the same fundamental cause.

Having examined the general natural population growth trends in the Delgany area between 1666 and 1779 the details of this population change in terms of the seasonality of the baptisms, marriages and burials will now be considered.[29] Figure 8 shows a monthly aggregation of all baptisms, marriages and burials recorded in the registers between 1666 and 1819. It can be seen that January, April, May and July were popular months for baptisms with March the most popular month of all. Burials peaked in late winter and in the spring months and were particularly common in January, March and May and at their highest in April. Burials were least frequent during the months of August and October.

Of the three events it is the burial seasonality which tells us least about a society. While people can choose the timing of a baptism or marriage, a burial must follow closely after death leaving little scope for choice with regard to the timing of the burial. As could be expected, therefore, the burial seasonality in the Delgany area is similar to the trends that have been found in other parishes. Lesley Bradley, for example, found from the study of the seventeenth and eighteenth century records of twelve parishes in Derbyshire and Nottinghamshire that burials peaked in spring and, persisting into April, dipped in summer and early autumn and peaked again, unlike in Delgany, in October. Bradley found August and September to be the least common month for burials.[30] This observed trend is easily explained in terms of burials peaking during the harshest months of the year.

The baptism pattern in the Delgany records also closely matches that of the English parishes studied by Bradley. Bradley found that baptisms peaked during February, March or April with March the most favoured month.[31] The autumn peak occurred in October or November with a dip in baptisms during August. As can be seen from figure 8, baptisms in the Delgany area dipped in August and remained low in September, moving upwards again in October, November and December.

Bradley has speculated on the causes of seasonality in baptisms and points out that historically baptisms can have been influenced by factors other than conception. What factors could have impacted on the timing of baptisms in the Delgany area? It has been seen that grain growing was an important agricultural pursuit in the region as early as the 1630s. By its nature, this type of farming had a very high requirement for labour during the harvest period that could not be postponed on a whim. There was a fine line between starvation and plenty and no farmer could afford not to harvest his crop if it was ripe and the weather was suitable. Caroline Brettell has shown the important role that female labour played in the agricultural economy of north-western Portugal.[32] So too was female labour vitally important during the autumn in arable areas of pre-industrial Ireland. The harvest had to be gathered and women were required to play their part. It is not immediately obvious, therefore, whether the August through October dip in baptisms was a manifestation of people choosing to delay baptisms until the harvest was over or was actually a case of couples planning the conception of children so that the birth would not fall during the harvest period. Unfortunately there is no evidence in the registers as to the age of children baptised in the eighteenth century.[33] However, if it were the case that the baptism of children born during the harvest season was habitually postponed, then it is reasonable to expect that figure 8 would show a baptism peak in November or December as the seasonal demand for labour fell away. Clearly this is not the case as the number of baptisms increased only slightly during these months.

It seems more feasible, therefore, to presume that family planning factors reduced the level of conceptions in the November to January period so as to reduce births between August and October. With wages increasing during the harvest, the opportunity cost of a woman's labour being unavailable at harvest time due to childbirth would have been great indeed.[34] In support of this idea, when the timing of marriage is considered in the next chapter, it will be seen that people did plan their lives to fit the natural seasonal rhythms of the area in which they lived. Figure 14 shows that marriages in the Delgany area were rare during the autumn months because people could not afford to take the time off from earning high harvest wages to marry. If people were prepared to postpone a marriage because the cost of losing a day's wages was too great then it seems plausible that they would plan conceptions so that women would not be indisposed for the entire harvest period.

Figure 8 shows clearly that there was a distinct annual rhythm to life in north-east Wicklow during the eighteenth century. However, by focussing too closely on the seasonal trends, one can easily be distracted from the traumatic events that impinged on the rhythms of life. Periodic epidemics could temporarily disrupt the rhythmic curves shown in figure 8 and people had to find a way to adjust to survive these unexpected demographic shocks. The largest monthly burial figure recorded between 1666 and 1819 occurred in June 1777 when twelve people were buried. In statistical terms, however, June should have been one of the months of fewest deaths but the twelve burials during June 1777 represented one third of all burials recorded that year. In table 14 the number of burials in 1746 and 1777 are shown. We have seen earlier that burials reached an all time high in 1746. However, in contrast with 1777, even though the burial figures were roughly the same for these two years, burials occurred regularly throughout 1746 rather than peaking during one particular month. Thus, although burials during 1746 were running at a particularly high level, the fundamental annual burial pattern remained the same during that crisis year.

Table 14   Burials during 1746 and 1777

Year	Jan	Feb	Mar	Apr	May	Jun	Jul	Aug	Sep	Oct	Nov	Dec	Total
1746	4	4	3	4	2		4	5	1	3	3	4	37
1777	2	3	2	4	3	12	1	4		2	2	1	36

Although aggregating baptisms and burials over a century and a half allows us to overcome the difficulties presented by short-term fluctuations in the seasonal pattern, it is these very short-term fluctuations that are the statistical manifestation of the sudden shocks that were referred to above. By aggregating monthly burials between 1666 and 1819 we have succeeded in minimising the statistical impact of the twelve burials that occurred during June 1777 on the long-term monthly burial trend. However, the people living in the Delgany area in the 1770s experienced this crisis month and had to struggle to survive through it. To ignore such short-term fluctuations, therefore, is to paint a false picture of social life in the area in the eighteenth century.

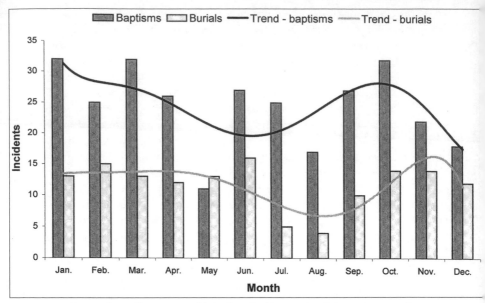

9. Seasonality of baptisms and burials in Delgany union between 1700 and 1719

In the thesis on which this study is based the aggregations of baptisms and burials in six different two-decade periods between 1700 and 1819 are presented and the graphs for the periods 1700–19, 1740–59 and 1800–19 are

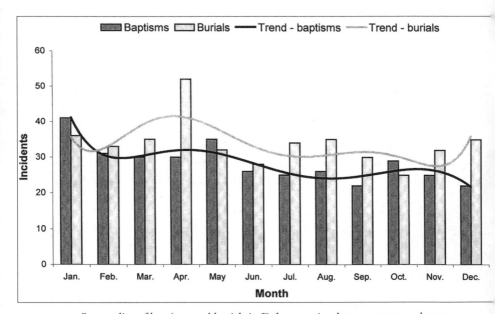

10. Seasonality of baptisms and burials in Delgany union between 1740 and 1759

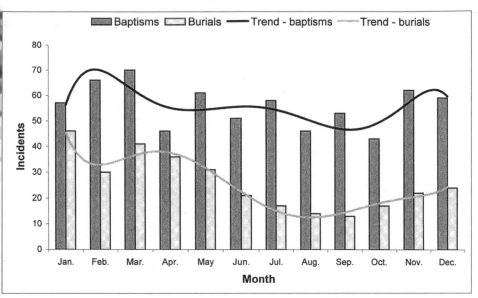

11. Seasonality of baptisms and burials in Delgany union between 1800 and 1819

shown here in figures 9, 10 and 11.[35] As can be seen in these three figures, various different patterns of baptisms and burials were experienced between these years, which when combined helped produce the smooth rhythmic pattern shown in figure 8.

Despite the variations in the above graphs, however, the basic rhythm of life appears to have remained fairly unchanged between 1700 and 1819. Throughout this entire period baptisms peaked in spring (usually March or April) and in autumn (September) whereas burials peaked in early spring. Both baptisms and burials dipped in autumn, usually in August. Between 1700 and 1719 baptisms were at their highest in March and October.[36] A century later the spring peak also occurred in March, while the autumn peak occurred in November. Burials in the 1700–19 period peaked in February and June and dipped in August whilst in the 1800–19 period they peaked in January and again dipped in August and October.

The 1740–59 period was earlier suggested to have been distinctive and unique. However, the seasonal pattern of baptisms and burials presented in figure 10 suggests that this period was perhaps not as unusual as may have been presumed. Certainly, burials were at an all time high during this period and the natural rate of population growth in the area was negative. However, the life rhythms appear to closely match that experienced during the other two-decade periods between 1700 and 1819.[37] Burials during the 1740s and 50s peaked in April, which closely corresponds to the general aggregate (figure 8) while baptisms peaked in January, a little earlier in the year than would be expected. Baptismal and burial nadirs occurred in September and October

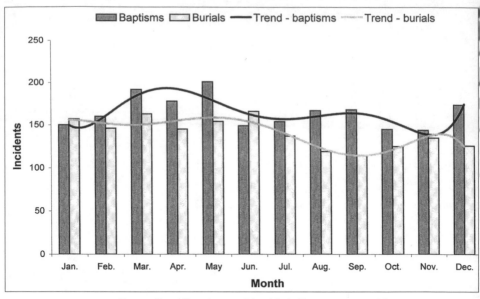

12. Seasonality of baptisms and burials in Powerscourt parish
between 1760 and 1849

respectively, again in keeping with the general trend. Thus, although the period
may have been characterised by high levels of mortality and reduced baptisms,
nonetheless the underlying rhythm of life remained substantially unchanged.

Some interesting similarities and differences emerge when the seasonality of
baptisms and births in Delgany is compared with both Bray and Powerscourt. In
general, the rhythm of life evident in both the Bray and Powerscourt eighteenth-
century parish records is quite similar to that of the Delgany. In Bray between
1760 and 1839 baptisms peaked in March and reached were lowest in July. In
contrast with Delgany, however, August was a fairly busy period for baptisms
perhaps suggesting that female labour was less important at this time of year in
the more urbanised Bray area. In the next chapter it will be seen that the lesser
dependence on high harvest-time wages in Bray produced a completely different
trend in the timing of marriage in Bray than in the Delgany parishes. Burials in
Bray were highest in January and were lowest in October.[38]

Figure 12 plots the seasonality of baptisms and burials in the pastoral parish
of Powerscourt between 1760 and 1849. In Powerscourt baptisms peaked in
the months of March, April and May, with May being the absolute peak, and
also in December. Baptisms were lowest in October and November.
Surprisingly the burial peak occurred very late in the year, in June. It is
possible that the burial peak in June says more about the quality of the
recording in the registers than about the seasonal rhythms in the parish. The
nadir for burials occurred, as in Delgany, in August and September.

The rhythms of the home: Family life in the Delgany union, 1666–1779

About [Newtown] Mount Kennedy the country is inclosed with various mountains and high lands. There are considerable tracts of mountain land improved ... Tithes are paid by composition. The crops are viewed and they agree for one year. The people increase much. Farms much taken in the mountains by partnership. Three or four will take 100 acres and divide among themselves as in Kilkenny. They have plenty of potatoes. All keep a cow, some more. Their fuel is turf from the mountains. They are universal pilferers of everything they can lay their hands on. Great liars, but full of quickness and sagacity, and grateful to excess.[1]

In the previous chapter it was seen that there was a distinct annual rhythm to life in north-east Wicklow in the seventeenth and eighteenth centuries with baptisms and burials peaking in late spring and dipping between the months of August and October. It was argued that the population change in an area over time could be viewed as an aggregation of the effects of the natural (fertility related) population change and the non-fertility related population change in the area during the period in question. In general the 1666–1819 period was seen as one of natural population growth. However, during the period 1720–70, natural population growth slowed and during the 1740s and 1750s natural population growth was negative.

In this chapter the mechanics of population change in the Delgany union between 1666 and 1779 will be studied in greater detail with particular attention being paid to the distinction between natural and non-fertility related change. Furthermore, in an effort to get an understanding of what everyday life was like for the people living in the area in the seventeenth and eighteenth centuries, other periodic rhythms that impacted on and influenced their way of life will be examined.

Historically, natural population change was strongly influenced by the average age at which women became sexually active. Thus, if one wishes to study the natural population change in an area, it is important to determine this variable as closely as possible. From an analysis of the parish registers it is clear that the vast majority of children in the area at this time were born into families where the father and mother were married as a maximum of twenty-four (and possibly as few as ten) of the 1,827 baptisms (*c.* 1 per cent) recorded between 1666 and 1779 were of children born out of wedlock.[2] It also seems to have been the case that if a child was born to unmarried parents the couple quickly *legitimised* the pre-marriage conception or birth by marrying either before or after the birth of the child (figure 13). Even if we accept that the parish incumbent may have been reluctant to either baptise or record the baptism of these children all evidence suggests that regular sexual intercourse between couples in the Delgany area, during the period under study, did not commence until after the relationship was legitimised by marriage. Thus, the age at which a woman commenced sexual intercourse was directly linked to the age of marriage of the woman and was probably contemporaneous with the marriage itself.

A second important factor influencing the natural rate of population increase was the average interval between successive births in a family. For instance, if the average age of marriage of a woman was sixteen and the average birth interval was two years, then a *typical* woman would have borne twelve children by her fortieth birthday. If, however, the average birth interval was three years and the average age of marriage for a woman was twenty, then only seven children would be born before the mother reached forty. As can be seen from this simple example, the combination of average age of marriage and average duration between successive births strongly influenced the birth rate and the size of families and hence the general population level.

The principal problem associated with the study of the Delgany union marriage registers is that only 188 marriages were recorded between 1666 and 1779 and it is consequently difficult to form definitive conclusions from events that occurred on average less than twice a year.[3] As was noted previously, the number of incidents of marriage are so low that it is virtually impossible to determine whether periods of two or three years during which no marriages were recorded represent gaps in the recording of marriages or genuine dearths. Nonetheless, examination of the marriage records does produce some significant and interesting population-change influencing information.

Unfortunately the typical marriage entry is not particularly informative and does not contain any indication of the age of either spouse. Hence, the age of marriage of a bride must be determined by calculating the gap between her baptism and her marriage. In the previous chapter it was seen that seventeenth and eighteenth-century records do not contain any indication of the time period between birth and baptism. However, when the recording in the baptismal records of dates of birth commenced in the early nineteenth century the average birth-baptism interval was of the order of fifteen days. Thus, in the absence of any definitive data for the seventeenth and eighteenth centuries, it seems reasonable to presume that the baptism of a child closely followed the birth date and that the gap between the baptism and the marriage closely reflects the age of marriage of the bride.

There are a number of problems with this approach, however. Firstly, as people were legally restricted from marrying before their sixteenth birthday no age of marriage figures can be determined for marriages celebrated before 1692. This is because the gap in recordings between 1675 and 1691 means that the baptism of a bride who married before 1675 would predate the commencement of baptismal records in 1666. So, of the 188 marriages listed in the records it is impossible to determine the age of marriage of the female partner for the twenty-six marriages recorded before 1692. In addition, many of the brides who married between the years 1692 to about 1715 would have been baptised between 1675 and 1692 (i.e. during the gap in recording) and the age of marriage of these women also cannot be determined. A further difficulty in the determination of the age of marriage of a bride is that she may not have been baptised in the parish or her baptism may have not been recorded. The Delgany marriage records show that the parish boundary was not an impediment to movement and that people married into families in the surrounding parishes and further afield. In one case Letice Keightly, born into a prominent family in the area, married Thomas Hammond from Norway.[4]

Of the 188 marriages recorded before 1779 the age of marriage (baptism/marriage interval) can be determined for only forty-eight brides.[5] Obviously one must be cautious about using such a small sample to deduce general age of marriage trends. Nonetheless even with this small sample size certain trends are clearly evident. For the entire period, the average age of marriage of the forty-eight brides is twenty-three years and seven months. However, if the average age of marriage is determined for each of the decades of the 1690s through to the 1770s, some significant differences emerge.

Table 15   Average age of marriage during the various decades between 1690 and 1779

Decade	Average age of marriage (years, months)	Number of known baptism-marriage intervals
1690s	21y 09m	4
1700s	23y 10m	2
1710s	18y 05m	6
1720s	21y 11m	12
1730s	20y 03m	2
1740s	20y 04m	8
1750s	30y 02m	5
1760s	25y 00m	5
1770s	21y 04m	4
1690s–1780s	23y 07m	48

In table 15 the calculated average age of marriage is shown on a decade-by-decade basis with the third column showing the number of marriages from which the various figures have been calculated.[6] Obviously, the more marriages one is dealing with, the more representative will be the calculated figure. Thus, the average age of marriage figures calculated for the decades of the 1700s and 1730s can be ignored because in both instances the age of marriage can be determined for only two brides.

As can be seen from table 15, the average age of marriage during the 1710s and the 1740s appears to have been especially low whereas during the 1760s and particularly the decade of the 1750s the average age of marriage was high. It is interesting that the 1750s appear to be the decade during which women married very late because it was found in the previous chapter that the 1740s and 1750s were the decades of negative natural population growth. While the average age of marriage figure for the 1750s may not be entirely accurate, because of the small amount of data from which the figures have been calculated, the suggestion that the typical bride was over thirty years old would assist in explaining the drop in baptisms (births) that occurred in the mid-eighteenth century. In general, early marriage was a feature of life for women in seventeenth and eighteenth century Delgany. Of the forty-eight marriages for which age of marriage can be calculated, twenty of these, or 41 per cent, were of women who were less than twenty years of age and five of the forty-eight brides were in their sixteenth year. The youngest known brides were Catherine Seymour who married in October 1710 and Jane Newton of Tinnapark, both of whom had been baptised just sixteen years, four months previously.

However, even if a woman did not marry early, it did not mean that she was necessarily excluded from marriage. There are five known instances of brides aged thirty or over. The oldest brides for whom an age of marriage is calculable were Elizabeth Bryan who was aged thirty-five and Anne Grundy who was thirty-eight.[7] These late marriages must surely have been conceived more for convenience and comfort than for child bearing. John Demos has found that marriage, or more particularly remarriage, in Plymouth Colony was often a case of compromise, with a widower with a young family remarrying swiftly so that his children could be reared while he worked the land.[8] Perhaps similar considerations lay behind these late marriages in Delgany. Certainly, when Anne Grundy married Anthony Ball, it seems unlikely that they hoped to produce a large family. There is little evidence of the type of remarriage that Demos noted in Plymouth Colony occurring in the Delgany area, there being only one definite instance of the remarriage of a widower in the records. Jarvis Boswell, from Kilincarrig, married Mary Darbishire in January 1675 and in February 1696 their second child, John, was baptised.[9] Mary died the following May leaving Jarvis to rear two children under five years of age.[10] Thus it was that, after little more than a year, Jarvis (Gervais) married Grace Hornby and they had two more children by September 1715.[11] It seems to have been common during the period under study to call a child after a brother or sister who had died previously. Mary Boswell's youngest son, John, also died in June 1696, just a week after his mother's death, and hence the first child born to Jarvis and Grace was called John, in remembrance.[12]

A second marriage-related factor that impacted on population trends is the average interval between marriage and the birth of the first child. Indeed this interval can tell quite a bit about attitudes to marriage in the area in the seventeenth and eighteenth centuries. If the interval is small this can be taken as evidence that, in deference to the case of Ball and Grundy's marriage of convenience, marriage was entered into for the purpose of raising a family.

The 'marriage–first birth interval' for Delgany has been determined by searching the baptismal records for the first recorded baptism of a child resulting from each of the 188 listed marriages. For the purposes of determining this interval, it has again been assumed that a child was baptised soon after birth, which may, of course, not have been the case and any delay in baptising the first child in a marriage will exaggerate the calculated marriage-first birth interval. Furthermore, some of the problems cited in calculating the average age of marriage also arise in the determination of the marriage-first birth interval. Many of the married couples did not settle in the parish and consequently the baptism of their children is not recorded in the records. Also, if either the first child was not baptised in the parish or if the first baptism was not recorded but subsequent baptisms were, then the marriage-first birth interval will be exaggerated. It has been possible to calculate the marriage-first birth interval for eighty-three of the 188 marriages with intervals ranging from less than six months to more than sixteen years.[13] There was only one instance of a child being born to a couple before they married. Intervals of more than five years are suspiciously long and are probably inaccurate and the four intervals that were calculated as exceeding ten years are almost certainly a result of either poor registration or previous children having been baptised in another parish.

In figure 13, the duration between marriage and first birth is shown for the eighty-three marriages for which the data is available. It is immediately clear from the graph that the majority of couples bore a child within eighteen months of their marriage. More specifically, over 55 per cent of these marriages presented a child for baptism between nine and eighteen months after the marriage and more than a quarter of the couples bore a child between nine and twelve months after the marriage. From this it can be concluded that marriage was seen primarily as a means by which children could be conceived and a lineage perpetuated. An interesting point about the marriage-first birth interval graph shown in figure 13 is that a second peak occurred in the third year of marriage with over 7 per cent of the marriages having a first child baptised between two years three months and two years six months after the marriage. The only plausible explanation for this second peak is that this must represent the second child born to most of these couples and that the first child either died before baptism or was not recorded in the

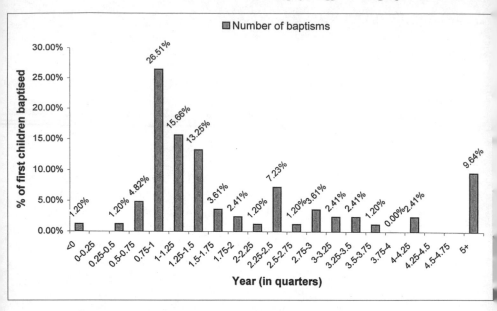

13. Duration after marriage when the first child was born to couples whose
marriages were recorded in the Delgany union, 1666–1779
(assuming a contemporary birth and baptism)

registers. It is extremely unlikely that as high a proportion as 7 per cent of
marriages actually bore a first child this long after the marriage.

During the 1666–1779 period there was a noticeable fluctuation in the
marriage–first birth interval. By excluding the larger intervals of five years or
more,[14] the average marriage–first birth interval has been calculated for four
periods between 1666 and 1779. These various intervals are listed in table 16.[15]

Table 16 Interval between marriage and baptism of first child for four
periods between 1666 and 1779

Period	Average interval (year/month) between marriage and first birth	Number of known marriage–first birth intervals
1666–99	1y 5m	22
1700–24	1y 7m	32
1725–59	1y 2m	11
1760–79	1y 5m	10

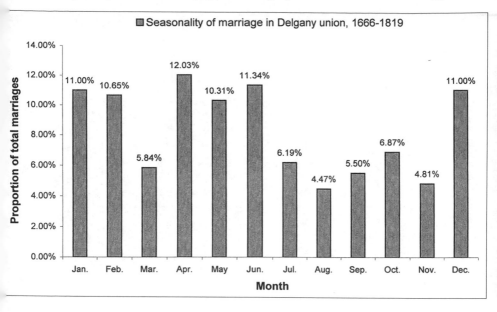

14. The aggregate number of marriages per month in the
Delgany union, 1666–1819.

The figures for the 1725–59 and 1760–79 periods may be less accurate than
the two earlier periods because they are calculated from smaller amounts of
data. However, it is interesting that the period 1725–59 is the time when the
shortest average interval between marriage and the baptism of a child occurs
because it was seen earlier that the 1750s was the decade during which average
age of marriage of the bride was at its highest. Perhaps these older brides were
more anxious to start a family at the earliest opportunity.

In the previous chapter discernible rhythms were observed in the baptism
and burial patterns with incidents of both peaking in late winter and early
spring and dipping between August and October. Although there are too few
marriage records to make a similar comparison, a periodic rhythm is evident
in the case of marriages if incidents of marriage are aggregated over a longer
period. Figure 14 shows the proportion of total marriages in the Delgany
union that were performed during each of the twelve months between 1666
and 1819 and figure 15 shows similar information for Bray and Powerscourt.[16]

Anne Kussmaul has found that in pre-industrial rural England people
married when they were not preoccupied with work and in her study she
identified links between the time of year when people married and the
general agricultural and industrial practices in the surrounding area.[17] In non-
industrial societies economic activity is governed by the seasons. Whereas
factors such as soil quality and market demand may influence the type of

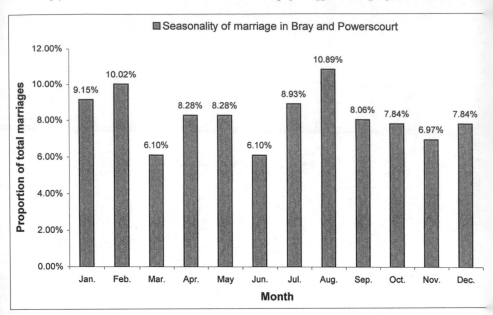

15. The aggregate number of marriages per month in the Bray union, 1666–1834 and Powerscourt parish, 1662–1853.

agriculture practised in a region it is the seasons that dictate the busy periods for the various agricultural activities. In grain-producing regions crops ripen during the autumn and historically wages tended to increase during the months of August to October when work was plentiful and hence marriages did not take place at this time.[18] Even urban dwellers in predominantly arable regions were not divorced from the seasonal influence. As vast amounts of labour were required to harvest the crop, workers were often attracted from towns into the countryside to share in the bounty.[19] Pastoral regions display a different and less specific rhythm. Lambs and calves were usually born during the spring so that the animals could be strengthened on fresh grass and as a result labour requirements increased moderately at this time of year.[20] However, dairying and cattle fattening were less seasonal and so required constant levels of labour for much of the year and as a consequence marriages in pastoral areas tended to be more evenly spread throughout the year.[21]

In north-east Wicklow the parishes of Bray and Powerscourt differed greatly in terms of agricultural practice from the parishes of the Delgany union and in particular from the parishes of Delgany and Kilcoole. Delgany, Kilcoole and Newcastle parishes comprise flat, fertile, coastal land and in the seventeenth and eighteenth century were areas of mixed farming with high levels of grain cultivation. By contrast, Powerscourt and Kilmacanoge parishes, more undulating, were primarily areas of cattle and sheep rearing.[22] Bray parish, on the other hand, while not dominated by the town, was more urban and industrialised than the neighbouring areas even as far back as the 1660s.[23]

One might thus expect the marriage profile of the Delgany union to differ from that of Bray and Powerscourt as is indeed the case. The Delgany union marriage profile (figure 14) is precisely what would be expected of an arable region in the seventeenth and eighteenth centuries. August was the least popular month for marriages between 1666 and 1819, during which only 4.5 per cent of all marriages were performed. In the previous chapter August was also found to have been the least common month for baptisms and burials. The five months of July through November witnessed only a little over a quarter of all recorded marriages (28 per cent). The most popular period for marrying was during the winter and in the late spring and early summer period when work would have been scarce. During the months of April through June over a third of all marriages were celebrated.

In sharp contrast, August was the most popular month for marriage in the parishes of Powerscourt and Bray (figure 15) and there is no discernible pattern to marriage trends in these non-arable parishes where the quantity of work was less influenced by the seasons. Marriages could be celebrated whenever one wished with little or no opportunity cost in terms of forfeited wages.

A common link between the two graphs, however, is that a dip in marriages occurred during March. Less than 6 per cent of the total marriages recorded in Delgany between 1666 and 1819 were performed during this month while in Bray and Powerscourt the proportion was only slightly higher. This mid-spring dip is accounted for by the fact that the Lenten period was one of the prohibited periods during which marriage was discouraged.[24] Fifty-four marriages for which the date of the marriage is known were performed during February, March or April between 1666 and 1779.[25] Only eight of these marriages (15 per cent) occurred during Lent. By contrast, sixteen of the fifty-four marriages (30 per cent) were performed either two days before the commencement or two days after the conclusion of Lent. The fact that 15 per cent of the total occurred within the forty-six day period of Lent whilst 30 per cent occurred in the four days on either side of Lent is conclusive proof that marriage during Lent was generally avoided.

Kussmaul has also found that marriages were often crowded into Christmas (and Easter) holidays when there was little work to be done so that the impact of the marriage on earnings would be kept to a minimum.[26] A tendency to marry during the Christmas holidays is unmistakably evident in the Delgany registers. In figure 14 December was shown to be the most popular month by far for marriage in the second half of the year. Table 17 lists the twenty December marriages for which the exact date of marriage is known.

The tendency to marry during the holiday period is obvious from table 17. Six of the twenty marriages (30 per cent) were celebrated within two days of

Christmas and eleven (55 per cent) within four days, thus minimising the opportunity cost of the celebration.

Two other key influences affecting population size are the average interval between successive births in a family and the rate of mortality in the community. As before, certain factors, principally relating to uncertainty as to the extent of under-recording of baptisms and burials, prevent an exact determination of either fertility or mortality. For instance, if we take a fairly typical case of a couple who married and had a child baptised within the year, if there is no further record of children being baptised to this couple, what does this imply? It is possible that the couple only had the one child. However, it is also possible that the couple emigrated from the area and raised a multi-child family in another area or that subsequent baptisms of their children within the parish were not recorded. If the couple only had the one child, why was this? Did the mother die in childbirth and her burial go unrecorded in the registers or was it simply the case that they did only have the one child? If, on the other hand, subsequent baptisms of the couple's children were not recorded,

Table 17 A list of all December marriages in the Delgany union, 1666–1779

Groom	Bride	Marriage Date	Christmas	
			Within 2 days of . . .	Within 4 days of . . .
James Reading	Dina Martin	26/12/1667	Yes	Yes
Peter Steephens	Ann Compson	12/12/1692		
John Holmes	Alice Bullard	27/12/1693	Yes	Yes
Emanuel Adams	Hanna Mason	31/12/1695		
Thomas Burfield	Dorothy Bath	16/12/1697		Yes
Edward Elliot	Mary Lambe	29/12/1697		Yes
John Boyle	Ann Plant	28/12/1699		
Thomas Livesley	Elizabeth Martin	11/12/1701		
William Rylands	Cisly Summers	15/12/1701		
John Elliott	Mary Seymor	26/12/1702	Yes	Yes
Samuel Oakes	Sarah Norton	29/12/1720		Yes
Paul Smith	Mary Anderson	26/12/1704	Yes	Yes
Michael Bryan	Elizabeth Doyle	12/12/1714		
William Revell	Mary Fox	27/12/1716	Yes	Yes
Joseph Harrisson	Dorothy Burfeild	20/12/1717		
John McAdams	Mary Smith	06/12/1722		
James Massey	Catherine Lyons	21/12/1722	Yes	
John Groods	Mary Sommers	29/12/1725	Yes	
Thomas Walker	Anne Fox	17/12/1764		
Thomas Hoare	Mary Edwards	24/12/1776	Yes	Yes

was this because they died before baptism (infant mortality), because they were not actually baptised or because the parish minister carelessly omitted them? Although these questions remain unanswered, some significant population trend information can be garnered from the baptism and burial registers.

One of the larger families occurring in the records is that of James and Elizabeth Bunn who must have married in the mid-1750s although their marriage is not recorded in the registers.[27] This family is worth analysing in detail because it illustrates many of the challenges faced by people in Delgany in the eighteenth century. By the 1750s, Bunns had been living in the area for generations and almost a century earlier John Bunn of Leamore in Newcastle parish had paid 2*s.* hearth-tax. John and Elizabeth's first child, John, was baptised in January 1757 and a second son was baptised the following December.[28] In all, fourteen Bunn children were baptised in the eighteen years between January 1757 and July 1775.[29] Two of the children, Sophia and Jane, were baptised on the same day and, although not explicitly stated in the records, were probably twins. The longest interval between baptisms for the family was the two years and nine months between the baptism of these twins on 4 September 1770 and Sarah on 16 June 1773. The shortest gap between baptisms is the eleven months and one day between the first two children born to James and Elizabeth. In all, the gap between three sets of baptisms was less than one year and the gap between eight sets of baptisms was less than two years.

Occasionally in the baptism records, a child will be described as having been 'privately baptis'd', a procedure which was performed if the child was sick and death was imminent. Mary Bunn was privately baptised on 11 April 1760 and was buried two days later. Four of the fourteen Bunn children appear in the burial records before they had reached the age of two.[30] The tendency to name a child after a previous son or daughter who had died earlier can also be seen. Joseph Bunn died in July 1767 aged one year eleven months and another son was called Joseph in 1775.

As has been stated, it is difficult to make an accurate estimate of the number of children born to a family unit in the late seventeenth and eighteenth centuries. This is because a majority of recorded baptisms are to family units that seem to have had only one child. However, a preponderance of one-child families must surely be an inaccurate reflection of real life in the area in the late seventeenth and eighteenth centuries. If the Delgany records are to be believed, of the 1,827 baptisms recorded in the registers between 1666 and 1779, more than half of the family units were one-child families (see figure 16) and the average number of baptisms per family unit was only 2.28 per family. Even if the one-child families were to be excluded from the calculation the average number of baptisms per family is still on the low side, at 3.81.

What figure 16 does show conclusively, however, is that large families were quite common in the Delgany area in the period under study and that over 9 per cent of families had six or more children baptised. Since inevitably some

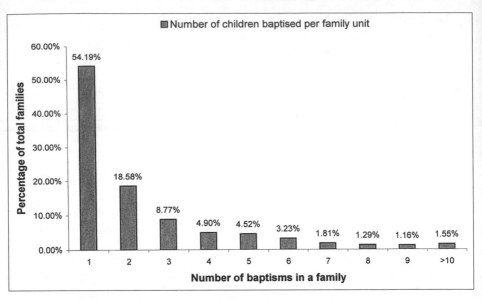

16. Proportionate distribution of baptisms per family unit.

baptisms must have been omitted from the records it can be concluded that this estimate for the proportion of total families that had more than six children is on the conservative side. The apparent preponderance of one-child families in the Delgany records may be because there were other churches in the immediate locality and it is probable that non-parishioners were sometimes baptised in Delgany church.

Since it is not possible to determine family size from the complete set of baptism records, we must find a representative sample of data for families that were definitely living in the area, so as to exclude inhabitants of the surrounding parishes from the estimate. The eighty-three families, used earlier for the purpose of determining the interval between marriage and the birth of the first child, are suitable for this purpose because the couples married in the parish and had at least one child baptised in Delgany, thus suggesting reasonably strong links with the area.[31] The results from this representative sample seem more realistic as the average number of children baptised per family unit exceeds three (3.2 baptisms per couple) while twenty-six of the eighty-three families (over 31 per cent) only had one baptism recorded. The number of baptisms-per-family figure from this sample is significantly higher and the proportion of one-child families much lower than was calculated from the complete set of data. This figure of 3.2 baptisms per couple would suggest that an average family size of 5.5 that was assumed in the first chapter is not excessive.[32]

It is the larger family units that are the most interesting and provide the best insight into the rhythms of family life in the Delgany area during the period

Table 18 Interval between baptisms in fifteen large family units

Family of	No. of children	Average interval (months) between baptism of their children	First child baptised	Last child baptised	Interval (year/month) between first and last baptism
Henry & Mary Banfield	9	24	15/11/1761	28/1/1778	16y02m
Richard & Anne Bruton	9	21	4/5/1751	26/6/1766	15y01m
James & Elizabeth Bunn	14 (incl. 1 set of twins)	17	5/1/1757	19/7/1775	18y06m
John & Mary Bunn	13	22	15/3/1722	17/4/1744	22y01m
John & Anne Edwards	11	29	4/1/1745	12/5/1769	24y04m
John & Sarah Elliott	9	25	10/4/1729	8/11/1745	16y07m
Thomas & Anne Fox	14 (incl. 1 set of twins)	22	31/5/1756	26/4/1778	22y00m
Thomas & Sarah Fox	11	20	7/1/1753	3/11/1769	16y10m
Thomas & Anne Fox	9	30	28/7/1700	27/12/1720	20y05m
John & Sarah Fox	9	30	4/4/1760	26/12/1779	19y09m
Joseph & Elizabeth Grundy	5	19	12/11/1715	25/2/1724	08y03m
Joseph & Elizabeth Grundy	9	26	29/2/1756	6/10/1774	18y07m
William & Elizabeth Keightley	9	18	29/12/1766	20/11/1778	21y11m
Nicholas & Elizabeth Seymour	9	21	23/3/1693	29/4/1707	14y01m
William & Frances Tuke	9	30	10/2/1704	3/5/1724	20y02m

under study. As we have seen, large families were common in the area between 1666 and 1779. In total, 107 families had five or more children baptised and the details of a random sample of these families are shown in table 18.

It seems to have been common for women to be either pregnant or nursing children for much of their married lives. In the sample of large families shown in table 18, there was a gap of more than twenty years between the baptism of the first and last child for five of the fifteen families. Anne Edwards must have had a particularly burdensome married life, bearing, as she did, eleven children stretching over a quarter of a century.

The interval between births (baptisms) varied quite considerably in these large families. James and Elizabeth Bunn's fourteen children were born in the space of eighteen years, with an average interval between births of one year and five months. Thomas and Anne Fox also produced fourteen children but over a period of twenty-one years and with an average birth interval exceeding one year and ten months. The shortest average interval between births in this sample is the year and five months for the aforementioned James and Elizabeth Bunn. It was not unusual for women to bear a child every eighteen to thirty months during their married childbearing years and the average interval between births for twelve of the fifteen families listed in table 18 falls within this range. Thus, the childbearing rhythm for many married women consisted of pregnancy followed by childbirth followed by nursing and quickly into another pregnancy cycle.

Having analysed some of the factors that impinge on natural population growth it is important to try to estimate the birth and death rates in the area during the seventeenth and eighteenth centuries. To estimate the birth and death rate of any population both the population level and the number of births and deaths must be known. However, since baptism and burial statistics for the Delgany area are only known for the Protestant community, these rates can only be estimated for Protestants rather than for the entire community.

In the first chapter population levels for Delgany, Kilcoole, Kilmacanoge and Newcastle parishes were noted for the years 1669, 1739, 1748 and 1766. While it was possible through surname analysis to estimate the Protestant proportion of the total population in 1669 from the hearth-money roll, the 1739 and 1748 figures are just house and hearth aggregates and contain no religious breakdown evidence. The 1766 census was conducted specifically to determine the religious breakdown in the country and thus estimates of the number of Protestants and Papists are available for the four parishes for that year. In the thesis on which this work is based, Protestant population estimates were derived for 1739 and 1748 (shown in table 19) based on the rather loose assumption that the Protestant proportion of the total population changed at a constant rate between 1666 and 1779.[33] Although this approach will mask any major inflows or outflows of population into the area, in the absence of any alternative religious breakdown estimates between 1669 and 1766, it is the only course available to us.

Using these Protestant population estimates, the baptism and burial rates can be estimated for various periods between 1669 and 1779. The rates have been estimated for a six-year period around each of the four years for which population estimates are available rather than for a specific year so that the calculations will not be skewed if a single year had an untypical number of baptisms or burials.

Table 19 Estimate of Protestant proportion of population of Delgany, Kilcoole, Kilmacanoge and Newcastle in 1669, 1739, 1748 and 1766

	1669			1739			1748			1766		
	Prots	Pop.	% Prot.	Prots	Pop.	% Prot.	Prots	Pop.	% Prot.	Prots	Pop.	% Prot.
Delgany	95	308	30.8	228	655	34.8	256	724	35.3	331	931	35.6
Kilcoole	258	677	38.1	226	963	23.4	221	1,025	21.5	200	1,161	17.2
Kilmacanoge	188	489	38.4	194	1,007	19.3	135	800	16.8	82	717	11.4
Newcastle	414	1,028	40.3	450	1,749	25.7	418	1,753	23.8	389	1,995	19.5
Total (incl. Newcastle)	954	2,502	38.2	1098	4,374	26.1	1030	4,302	24.6	1002	4,804	20.9
Total (excl. Newcastle)	541	1,474	36.7	648	2,625	26.4	612	2,549	25.1	613	2,809	21.8

Table 20 shows the aggregate baptisms and burials for four six-year periods centring on the years 1669, 1739, 1748 and 1766 and also the average annual baptism and burial levels during these six-year periods. The baptism and burial trends that were outlined in the previous chapter are immediately evident from this data. As is shown, high numbers of baptisms and low numbers of burials were recorded in the late 1660s-early 1670s indicating rapid population advance. Between the late 1730s and early 1750s, however, the natural population increase had become negative with average annual burials exceeding baptisms. By the mid-1760s positive natural population growth had again returned with both baptisms and burials running at a high level.

Table 20 Aggregate and average baptisms for various six-year periods between 1669 and 1779 (Newcastle figures included for 1667–72 period)

Period	Baptisms		Burials	
	Total	Avg. per year	Total	Avg. per year
1667–72	153	25.5	49	8.2
1737–42	80	13.3	96	16.0
1746–51	90	15.0	135	22.5
1764–69	170	28.3	159	26.5

Using these average annual baptism and burial figures in conjunction with the Protestant population estimates shown in table 19, baptism and burial rates per thousand people can be calculated. These rates are shown in table 21.

The data in table 21 strongly supports the demographic findings of the previous two chapters. The greatest differential between the baptism and burial rates occurred in the period 1667–72 supporting the proposition, made earlier,

Table 21 Baptism and burial rates for various periods between 1666 and
1779 for which Protestant population estimates are available

Period	Average baptisms per year	Average burials per year	Population (Newcastle included in 1667–72 figures)	Protestants Baptisms per 1,000	Burials per 1,000
1667–72	25.5	8.2	954	26.4	8.4
1737–42	13.3	16.0	648	20.6	25.0
1746–51	15.0	22.5	612	24.5	36.8
1764–69	28.3	26.5	613	46.2	43.2

that the age profile of the Protestant population at the time was low and that
young couples were having large families. The Bulkeley report had indicated
that there were few Protestants in the area in 1630 and so the high natural
population increase of the late 1660s supports the view that significant
Protestant migration into the area had occurred in the preceding decades. The
negative natural population growth that occurred in the 1740s is evident from
the burial rate exceeding the baptism rate in the 1737–42 and 1746–51
periods. By the mid-to-late 1760s natural population growth had again
become positive but the relatively high burial rate of 43 per thousand indicates
either a substantial aged population or perhaps regular demographic crises.

   The calculated baptism and burial rates are in the same ballpark as the
figures that David Eversley found for various Worcestershire parishes between
1705 and 1744.[34] Eversley calculated a baptism rate ranging from 35.79 per
thousand between 1705 and 1714 to 44.00 per thousand between 1735 and 1744.
These baptism rates are slightly higher than those calculated for Delgany with the
exception of the high baptism rate of the 1764–9 period. Worcestershire burial
rates ranged from 29.30 per thousand in the 1705–14 period to 37.34 per
thousand between 1730 and 1734 and the Delgany burial rates seem neither
exceptional nor unique when compared with Eversley's figures.[35]

   The impermanence of human life was something that the people of the
seventeenth and eighteenth century were deeply aware of. Death was a frequent
if unwelcome visitor that could unexpectedly steal away infants and adults, the
sick and the healthy, the poor and the rich. In the previous chapter a seasonal
rhythm was observed with regard to burials with them peaking in late winter
and early spring. However, this statistical view gave little indication as to how
the people may have felt about death. It is easy to allow oneself believe that
people were anaesthetised by the frequency of death to its deadly and brutal
permanence and graciously accepted the inevitably that periodic crises or
unforeseen illnesses would arise to strike down themselves or their acquain-
tances. Headstone-inscription analysis certainly points to this having been the

case.[36] There is a very marked difference between the inscriptions on the pre-nineteenth century headstones in the cemeteries at Delgany and Kilcoole as compared with post-1800 inscriptions. The inscriptions on the older headstones tend to relate *fact*, stating little more than the name, age and date of death of the deceased. Later headstones, by contrast, are more inclined to relate *emotion* and regularly refer to the deceased as 'beloved' and 'in loving memory of'. Two examples from Delgany cemetery suffice to illustrate this point.

Pre-1800 inscription
> 'Here lyeth ye bod^y/of Joshua Bell de/ceas^d August ye 10th/1733 aged 55 years/here also lieth ye bo^dy/of Mary Bell deceas^d/August 29th 1749 aged 53'[37]

Post-1800 inscription
> 'Erected by/Sarah Lawless of Delgany/in memory of her beloved husband/Mr James Lawless whe departed this/life Novr 15th 1868 aged 58 years/also four of their children who died young/also in loving memory of Sarah wife of the above/who departed this life the 13th Sept 1889/aged 80 years . . .'[38]

However a contemporary account of a funeral in Delgany in the 1790s gives a greater insight into late-eighteenth century attitudes to death and utterly contradicts any ideas we may have of an eighteenth-century ambivalence towards death.

> At the old church-yard of Delgany we saw a funeral, attended by a great concourse of young men and women. It was that of a young man, a linen-weaver, who was called to eternity before he had reached his twenty-ninth year. He left an aged mother, whom he supported, and a widow with five children. Who could refrain from shedding a tear over his early grave, when his wife stood wild and motionless there; grief choked [sic] her utterance. . . .[39]

It is clear from this account that families were not just affected emotionally by the death of a relative. In this case the widow may have been grieving less for her dead husband than for the perilous condition that the family now found itself in. Nonetheless her grief was real and heartrending. With the death of its breadwinner, a family was likely to be left destitute and reliant on the support of relatives or parish alms.[40] The Delgany poor list for 1716, for example, contained seven names, three of whom were widows.[41]

Child mortality was another event that was all too common in Delgany in the seventeenth and eighteenth centuries and was greatly feared. A traveller's account of a trip through Wicklow in 1791 illustrates this fear of infant mortality.[42] Describing the difficult and dangerous ascent to St Kevin's Bed in Glendalough, the author continues,

The ascent to this bed is not less difficult than the entrance and the prospect terrible, and yet we were informed of many women who underwent this desperate pilgrimage in the last month of their pregnancy. This ridiculous ceremony, is nevertheless considered by many of them as an infallible preservation against the fatalities of childbirth.[43]

The parish registers can be used to estimate the rate of infant mortality in the Delgany area between 1666 and 1779. For this purpose infant mortality will be presumed to encompass the deaths of all children who died before they reached the age of two. As with all conclusions that are made from parish records, it must be reiterated that an accurate estimate for infant mortality is greatly affected by the quality and completeness of the records. Table 22 shows the rate of infant mortality in the constituent parishes of the Delgany union for various periods between 1666 and 1777.[44]

A major problem in the determination of infant mortality rates is that the records only contain burials and baptisms that occurred within the union. Thus a child may have been baptised in Delgany church but buried in another parish or vice versa and such combinations of baptisms and burials will not be included in the infant mortality statistics. Also, these infant mortality statistics only include children that were actually baptised. Thus, for example, if stillborn children were not baptised (and it is not clear whether they were or not) they will not be included in the infant mortality estimates. However, while the estimates may not be entirely accurate, they are as accurate as the available information permits.

The infant mortality rates shown in table 22 give a further important insight into the mortality levels in the Delgany union that were outlined in the previous chapter. The 1740s and 1750s were undoubtedly years of great hardship and distress in the area and it was earlier speculated that a greying of the population occurred in the 1720s and 1730s which resulted in a falling birth rate and rising death rate in the 1740s and 1750s. From our infant

Table 22 Infant mortality rates in the Delgany union for
various periods between 1666 and 1777

Period	No. of baptisms	Number of children baptised in this period who died before 2 years of age two years	Percentage of total baptisms for which the child died within
1666–1700	387	22	5.7
1701–20	294	23	7.8
1721–40	302	27	8.9
1741–60	350	58	16.6
1761–77	491	41	8.4

mortality statistics, however, it is clear that a significant part of the increased numbers of deaths in the 1740s and 1750s were infant deaths. It is highly probable, therefore, that there was a linkage between the birth and death rate during these two decades. Newborn children had a lesser chance of surviving during this period, thus accounting for some of the increased death rate. However, since newborn children had a lesser chance of surviving, the people may have responded by having fewer children, resulting in a fall in the baptism rate. What cannot be answered, however, is whether this reduction in the baptism rate was a deliberate form of family planning or a natural reduction in fertility levels caused by prolonged distress. As will be seen, however, infant mortality peaked during the 1750s suggesting that society may have had difficulty in coping with the distress of the 1740s and 1750s.

The proportion of total deaths that were accounted for by the death of infants (less than two years of age) is shown in figure 17.[45] As can be seen, there was a wide fluctuation in the rate of infant deaths between these years and 1739, 1745 and 1751 emerged as particularly bad years. The reason for the high levels of infant mortality in 1739 and 1745 is unknown, as there are no other indications that either of these years were times of distress in the parish. However 1751 was a difficult year with burials (twenty-nine) at their highest level since 1746 and not being exceeded again until 1766.

As we have seen 1746 was a year of exceptionally high burials in the Delgany area. Yet figure 17 shows that only 13 per cent of these burials were accounted for by confirmed infant deaths and infant burials did not account

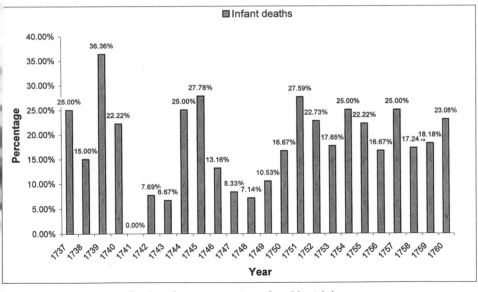

17. Infant burials as a proportion of total burials between
1737 and 1760 in the Delgany union.

for more 17 per cent of total burials in any year between 1746 and 1750. In the 1740s, a period of unprecedented high burial levels, infant burials accounted for only 13 per cent of total burials. However, during the 1750s when burials were less high, infant burials accounted for over 21 per cent of total burials. Clearly, therefore, the high infant mortality levels of the 1750s in particular adds weight to the idea, mentioned earlier, that prolonged distress over two decades may have affected the general health of the community.

Thus far this chapter has concentrated on analysing the parish registers to determine various aspects of natural (fertility-related) population change in the Delgany union between 1666 and 1779. However, as was discussed earlier, actual population change is determined by the combined influences of the natural and the non-fertility related population change. In order to form a complete understanding of actual population change in the Delgany area, it is necessary to formulate some impression as to the trends in, and the extent of, non-fertility related population change during this period.

Parish records by their nature contain information about the fundamentals of natural (fertility related) population change, namely marriages, baptisms (births) and burials (deaths). They are not an ideal source for the study of non-fertility related population change. However, in the absence of other sources for the levels of immigration into and emigration from an area, they are often the best that are available. Surname analysis of the parish registers, the baptism and burial records in particular, will give some indication of non-fertility related change in the region. Marriage records are less good in this regard because parishioners commonly married people from another parish or even of another religion. By enumerating the surnames occurring in the registers at particular times and looking for surname continuity over the years, periods of significant internal or external migration can be identified. The procedure used here consists of counting the occurrence of each unique surname in the baptism and burial records over successive periods of approximately twenty years. Such a long time period is necessary because a family can conceivably be living in an area and yet not appear frequently in the parish registers. Consider the case of a married couple that has completed their family, for example. After the baptism of their last child, no baptism or burial record concerning this family will be made until either a member of the family dies or one of their children present a child for baptism. Even during the twenty-year interval that has been suggested here either of these two events may not occur, even if the family has remained in the area. Thus, the results derived from a determination of non-fertility related population change from parish registers must be treated with some caution.

A further difficulty in using parish registers for the study of non-fertility related population change can be seen from the estimate that was made earlier in this chapter that over 50 per cent of family units appear to have had only one child baptised (figure 16). It was suggested that the preponderance of one-child families indicated a high degree of mobility between the Delgany union area and the surrounding parishes. Thus, an increased number of surnames appearing in the parish records during a particular period might be an indication of increased mobility between parishes rather than an increased population as a result of immigration and vice versa.

While accepting that there are numerous difficulties associated with using parish registers to analyse non-fertility related population change, a study of the Delgany registers does, nonetheless, indicate interesting trends and probable non-fertility related population change. In table 23 the number of unique surnames occurring in the Delgany baptism and burial records during selected periods is shown. Also, since the duration of the periods chosen vary, the number of unique surnames per year is shown so as to make comparisons between periods more meaningful.

As can be seen, an increase in the number of unique surnames (and the number of unique surnames per year) occurs between 1721–40 and 1741–60 and more markedly between 1741–60 and 1761–77. This suggests that internal migration may have been occurring in the latter half of the eighteenth century and particularly in the years between 1761 and 1777. In the previous chapter it was speculated that a greying of the population might have occurred in the 1740s and 1750s because of the fall in baptisms and increase in burials during these decades. It was also speculated that internal migration during the 1760s may have been responsible for the reversal of this marked demographic trend. The data shown in table 23 strongly supports this postulation.

Few surnames survived in the area from the 1660s to the 1770s. Those that do include Bryan, Bunn, Dalton, Darbyshire, Doyle, Elliott, Gilbert, Holmes, Kisby, Lamb, Mason, Massey, Matthews, Morgan, Norton, Quin, Wilkinson and Williams. The most frequently occurring surname in the records is Fox, occurring 117 times in the baptism records (6.4 per cent of all baptisms), 75 times in the burial records (5.5 per cent of all burials) and 19 times in the marriage records. Despite this the Foxes were not ancient inhabitants of the area[46] as the first occurrence of the surname in the registers records the baptism of John Fox in 1697.[47]

Table 23 Number of unique surnames occurring in the Delgany union baptism and burial records for various periods between 1666 and 1779

Period	No of years	No of unique surnames occurring in baptism and burial registers	Number of unique surnames per year
1666–75	10	97	9.70
1691–1700	10	89	8.90
1701–20	20	146	7.30
1721–40	20	167	8.35
1741–60	20	209	10.45
1761–77	17	301	17.71

Table 24 Occurrence of surnames in the Delgany union baptism & burial
records in successive periods between 1666 and 1777

Period	Total surnames	Number of surnames that occur in the next period	Proportion of surnames that occur in the next period
1666–75	97	17	17.53%
1691–1700	88	50	56.82%
1701–20	149	77	51.68%
1721–40	167	88	52.69%
1741–60	209	100	47.85%
1761–77	301	n/a	n/a

Determining the occurrence of surnames in the registers in two successive time periods can be seen as a measure of migration during the first period.[48] For example, if a surname occurs in one twenty-year period and is absent from the records in the next period then this family is likely to have moved out of the area. In table 24 the occurrence of surnames in the baptism and burial records in successive periods is shown.

The higher the number of surnames occurring in the next period (higher percentage figure in fourth column of table 24), the lower is the degree of external migration. Thus, as can be seen, the greatest mobility appears to have occurred between the 1666–75 and 1691–1700 periods. However, this can be explained by the gap in recording between 1675 and 1691, which means that the periods are not contiguous. As can be seen, mobility seems to have increased as the eighteenth century progressed.

Of the 167 unique surnames recorded between 1721 and 1740, only 88 of these or slightly more than 50 per cent recur in 1741–60. However, of the 209 unique surnames occurring in the registers between 1741 and 1760, less than half recur between 1761 and 1777. Despite the doubts we may have in using parish registers to find evidence of mobility for a particular area, the fact that the proportion of surnames during one period that recur in the next period falls as the eighteenth century progresses is surely a strong indication of increasing migration. Table 24 suggests that the area was most stable at the close of the seventeenth century with 57 per cent surname recurrence between 1691–1700 and 1701–20. By the 1741–60 period, only 48 per cent of surnames recorded recurred in the registers between 1761 and 1777. Thus, immigration into the three parishes seems to have become more common in the 1750s and 1760s. This finding strongly supports the suggestion made in the previous chapter that migration into the area commenced in the 1760s after two decades of falling baptisms and rising burials.

Conclusion

At its core this work is a study of various elements of population change that affected the parishes of Delgany and Kilcoole between the 1660s and the 1780s. During the course of the study, however, numerous sub-themes arose which required both analysis and explanation. And yet, how could it have been otherwise? What is the purpose of a population study if it does not concern itself with the everyday lives of the inhabitants of the area? Is not how people and communities responded to a changing environment a principal theme of local historical research? It is for this reason that the various population-influencing factors such as how the average age of marriage and the marriage-first birth interval may have varied over time and how baptisms, marriages and burials were affected by seasonality factors were investigated.

In the first chapter the general population trends in north-east Wicklow and south-east Dublin between 1660 and 1860 were examined. It was observed that the demographic makeup of the area had changed substantially in the three decades after 1630. In 1630 there were few Protestants in the area, Powerscourt parish excepted. By the 1660s, however, Protestants comprised a large proportion of the total population, a situation that continued until the publication of the first census containing religious figures in 1861. In general, the population was observed to have advanced between the 1660s and the 1830s with the exception of the 1740s when frequent demographic crises occurred.

In the second chapter these general population trends were verified by an analysis of the Delgany union registers. The registers also showed that the Protestant population continued to fall in the 1750s (figures 6 and 7), before increasing again probably as a result of the immigration of young married couples during the 1760s. The effects of distress on the baptism and burial rate were also examined and particularly 'difficult' years, when the burial rate increased to very high levels, were identified. Burials in 1746 reached an all time high figure of thirty-seven.

The inhabitants of the Delgany area, during the seventeenth and eighteenth centuries, were largely dependent on agriculture and their lives were greatly influenced by the seasons. A good harvest meant high wages and plenty whereas a poor harvest could often mean suffering and want. A key consideration of the second chapter, therefore, was the link between the seasonal trends of baptisms and burials in the area and the varying demand for labour. It was observed that the area illustrated a distinctive annual rhythm with both baptisms and burials peaking during the late-winter and early spring and dipping during the autumn. Although there is no definite proof, it is highly likely that the dip in baptisms during autumn was a result of controlled conception as families could not afford the opportunity cost of a nursing mother having to forfeit high harvest wages.

In the final chapter the parish registers were used to investigate many of the factors that influence population change. Fluctuations in the average age of marriage over time were observed and it was noted that the average age of marriage reached a peak in the 1750s, when natural population growth was negative. It was also observed that over 55 per cent of couples produced a child between nine and eighteen months after marriage. It can be inferred from this that marriage in the eighteenth century was viewed as an instrument by which a lineage could be perpetuated.

The seasonality of marriage was also investigated and it was seen that marriage during the harvest months was rare. Kussmaul has argued that this was because people could not afford to forego the high wage rates that were paid during the harvest in grain-producing areas. The pastoral parish of Powerscourt and the semi–urban parish of Bray did not exhibit this seasonality. It was seen, also, that marriages were regularly crammed into the holiday period around Christmas and Easter so that they would not impact on the wage earning potential of the guests.

The baptism and burial rates were estimated for four periods between 1666 and 1779 and were seen to confirm the population trends that were outlined in the earlier two chapters. Specifically, it was seen that the burial rate exceeded the baptism rate during the 1740s. Finally, non-fertility related population change was investigated and was found to support earlier suggestions that immigration had increased in the 1760s in the aftermath of the population contraction of the 1740s and 1750s.

The combined impact of the findings presented in this pamphlet gives us a good understanding of how the population of the Delgany area fluctuated between the 1660s and the 1780s and how the inhabitants responded to changing economic and social circumstances. However, the Delgany area should be viewed as just a small part of a bigger picture and there remains great scope for a population study of the entire north-east Wicklow region, encompassing the parishes of Powerscourt and Newcastle and the unions of Delgany and Bray. Such a population study would avoid the one major problem that was encountered throughout this study – namely the smallness of many of the data samples. By widening the scope of the research the biases and limitations in the Delgany registers would consequently be reduced.

Notes

ABBREVIATIONS

N.L.I.   National Library of Ireland
N.U.I.M.   National University of Ireland, Maynooth
H.C.   House of Commons
J.K.A.S.   *Journal of the Kildare Archaeological Society*
J.R.S.A.I.   *Journal of the Royal Society of Antiquaries of Ireland*
I.H.S.   *Irish Historical Studies*
D.P.R.1   *Delgany parish registers, book 1*
D.V.B.1   *Delgany vestry book, book 1*
R.C.B.   *Representative Church Body*

INTRODUCTION

1 Jacob Nevill, *An actual survey of the County of Wicklow*, copy of map published in Ken Hannigan and William Nolan (eds.), *Wicklow history and society*, (Dublin, 1994), inside back cover.

2 K. M. Davies, *Bray Irish historic towns atlas*, ix, (Dublin, 1999), p. 1.

3 Goddard H. Orpen, 'Novum Castrum McKynegan, Newcastle, County Wicklow' in *J.R.S.A.I.*, xxxviii, (1908), p. 129.

4 Lord Walter Fitzgerald, 'The manor and castle of Powerscourt, County Wicklow, in the sixteenth century, formerly a possession of the earls of Kildare' in *J.K.A.S.*, vi, no. 2, (1909–11), p. 127.

5 *The last county. The emergence of Wicklow as a county, 1606–1845* by County Wicklow heritage project, (Wicklow, 1993), p. 12.

6 Little Bray consisted of at least ten houses in 1664, G. S. Cary, 'Hearth money roll for Co. Dublin' in *J.K.A.S.*, xi, (1930–3), p. 458 while Great Bray consisted of at least

fourteen houses and Wicklow town at least one hundred houses in 1669, Liam Price, 'The hearth money roll for County Wicklow' in *J.R.S.A.I.*, lxi, (1931), p. 167 and p. 171.

7 Thomas Radcliff, *A report of the agriculture and livestock of the County of Wicklow, presented under the directions of the Farming Society of Ireland*, (Dublin, 1812), p. 2.

8 A 1636 Meath estate deed concerning Delgany refers to the presence of a 'Water-mill', N.L.I., microfilm p 2935.

9 William Wilson, *The post-chaise companion or, travellers directory, through Ireland*, (Dublin, 1784), column 194.

10 Radcliff, *A report of the agriculture and livestock of the County of Wicklow*, pp 37–38.

11 Robert Fraser, *General view of the agriculture and mineralogy, present state and circumstance of the County Wicklow, with observations on their means of improvement, drawn up for the consideration of the Dublin Society*, (Dublin, 1801), p. 68.

12 M. V. Ronan, 'Archbishop Bulkeley's Visitation of Dublin,

1630' in *Archivium Hibernicum*, viii, new series (1941), pp 81–85.

13 Samuel Lewis, *A topographical dictionary of Ireland* (2 vols, London, 1837), i, p. 450.

14 Judith Flannery, *Christ Church Delgany 1789–1990: Between the mountains and the sea*, (Delgany, 1990), p. 28.

15 G. S. Cary, 'Hearth money roll for Co. Dublin, 1664' in *J.K.A.S.*, x, (1922–8), pp 245–254 and G. S. Cary, 'Hearth money roll for Co. Dublin' in *J.K.A.S.*, xi, (1930–3), pp 386–466.

16 *Hearth money roll for Co. Wicklow 1669*, (N.L.I., Ms 8818) (also G.O. 667). Summary of this roll, naming all payees with more than one hearth published by Liam Price, 'The hearth money roll for County Wicklow' in *J.R.S.A.I.* lxi (1931), pp 164–78.

17 *Notes made by S. Lane-Poole . . . hearth money, 1739* . . (N.L.I., Ms 7227).

18 *Summary Vol. Dublin Diocese* (Religious Census) (N.A.I. M 2476 (i)).

19 *D.P.R.1.* In local custody.

20 Ann Kussmaul, *A general view of the rural economy of England 1538–1840*, (Cambridge, 1990), pp 14–18.

GENERAL POPULATION TRENDS IN
THE NORTH-EAST WICKLOW AREA
BETWEEN 1660 AND 1861

1 Down Survey parish maps, County Wicklow, *The Halfe Barony of Rathdowne In the County of Wicklow*, (N.L.I., Ms 726), unnumbered (microfilm p 7385).

2 Charles Varley (Varlo), *The unfortunate husbandman; an account of the life and travels of a real farmer in Ireland, Scotland, England and America*, ed. Desmond Clarke (Oldbourne, 1964), p. 70.

3 Down Survey parish maps, County Wicklow, *Halfe Barony of Rathdowne,* (N.L.I., Ms 726), unnumbered.

4 The 1813 census figures for Wicklow are just barony aggregates and contain no parish figures.

5 One reason for movement across the county boundary was related to the ecclesiastical organisation of the Church of Ireland parishes. As the Protestant parish of Bray (in Wicklow) was united with the Dublin parishes of Oldconnaught and Kiltiernan many people regularly travelled south from these Dublin parishes to attend church at Bray.

6 Seamus Pender, *Census of Ireland, circa 1659*, (Dublin, 1935), pp 381–2. Cary, 'Hearth money roll for Co. Dublin' in *J.K.A.S.*, xi, p. 457–8.

7 Ronan, 'Archbishop Bulkeley's Visitation', pp 56–98.

8 Ronan, 'Archbishop Bulkeley's Visitation', pp 81–5.

9 Pender, *Census of Ireland*, p. 610.

10 L. M. Cullen, 'Population trends in seventeenth-century Ireland' in *Economic and Social Review*, vi, no. 2, (1975), p. 153. William Smyth, 'Society and settlement in seventeenth-century Ireland: the evidence of the "1659 census"' in William J. Smyth and Kevin Whelan (eds.), *Common ground. Essays on the historical geography of Ireland*, (Cork, 1988), p. 56, suggests a multiplier of 2.5.

11 Petty (mid-seventeenth century) estimated 5 1/2 to a house, Gervase Parker Bushe, 'An essay towards ascertaining the population of Ireland' in J. Lee (ed.) *The population of Ireland before the nineteenth century*, (Germany, 1973), p. 151 whereas Bushe (late eighteenth century) estimated over

6.2 per house, Gervase Parker Bushe, 'An essay towards ascertaining the population of Ireland', p. 147.

12 The inland parish of Kiltiernan was significantly larger than the maritime Oldconnaught parish and yet Oldconnaught had a much larger population. A study of the '1659' figures for the baronies of Gorey and Ballaghkeen, Co. Wexford, also found that 'the population groups in 1659 were found in greater density along the Wexford seaboard and by the deep flowing rivers', Joseph Ranson, 'A census of Ireland c. 1659' in *The Past. The journal of the Ui Ceinnsealaigh Historical Society*, No. 4, 1948, p. 112.

13 Edward McLysaght, 'Seventeenth century hearth money rolls with full transcript relating to County Sligo' in *Analecta Hibernica*, xxiv, (1967), p. 1.

14 David Dickson, Cormac Ó Gráda and Seamus Daultry, 'Hearth tax, household size and Irish population change 1672–1821' in *Proceedings of the Royal Irish Academy*, lxxxii, C, No. 6, (Dublin, 1982), p. 139.

15 Dickson, Ó Gráda and Daultry, 'Hearth tax', p. 139.

16 McLysaght, 'Seventeenth century hearth money rolls', pp 13–14.

17 Cary, 'Hearth money roll for Co. Dublin, 1664' in *J.K.A.S.*, x, pp 245–254 and Cary, 'Hearth money roll for Co. Dublin' in *J.K.A.S.*, xi, pp 386–466 and Hearth money roll for Co. Wicklow 1669, (N.L.I., Ms 8818).

18 Brian Gurrin, 'Populating a parish. Changing population trends in the civil parishes of Delgany, Kilcoole and Kilmacanoge between 1666 and 1779', M.A. Thesis 1999,

N.U.I.M, pp 139–159; copies at Greystones and Maynooth Libraries. Hereinafter referred to as Gurrin, 'Populating a parish'.

19 Dickson, Ó Gráda and Daultry, 'Hearth tax' p. 149.

20 Davis, *Bray*, p. 15.

21 Gurrin, 'Populating a parish', pp 223–5.

22 This figure of 45 per cent is clearly a vast exaggeration. Since we are looking at the baptism records for a five-year period (1666–70), it is possible that a householder appearing in the records in 1666 died before 1669 and would thus not have been recorded in the hearth-tax roll. There are many instances of the same surname but different first names appearing in both the parish records and the hearth-money roll. Also, in many instances very similar names occur in both. Unless I am absolutely sure that I am dealing with the same person, I have assumed the persons to be different.

23 K. H. Connell, *The population of Ireland 1750 – 1845*, (Oxford, 1950), pp 4–5.

24 Fraser, *General view of the agriculture . . . of the County Wicklow*, p. 240.

25 In contrast with this county-wide estimate, a detailed survey of the Malton Estate in south Wicklow conducted before 1735 reported an average house size of less than 4.5. However since this survey focuses on an area quite distant from the Delgany region its significance is questionable; N.L.I. Ms. 6054, Survey of Lord Malton's Estate by Mr Hume.

26 Charles Henry Hull (ed.), *The economic writings of Sir William Petty together with the observations upon the bills of mortality*, (2 vols, Cambridge, 1899), i p. 141.

27 Calculated from table 4.

28 This point is developed more completely in Gurrin, 'Populating a parish', p. 30.

29 Gurrin, 'Populating a parish', pp 162–7.

30 This figure of 5.5 per household is supported by the baptism data in the parish registers. See Gurrin, 'Populating a parish', pp 30–1.

31 Gurrin, 'Populating a parish', p. 142 and pp 158–9.

32 See Gurrin, 'Populating a parish', pp 139–59 for a townland breakdown of the population and religious makeup of the parishes of Kiltiernan and Oldconnaught in 1664 and Bray, Powerscourt, Delgany, Kilcoole, Kilmacanoge and Newcastle in 1669.

33 Surname analysis of the 1669 hearth-money roll suggests that 38 per cent of the population of Kilcoole was Protestant. Yet the 1766 Religious Census reported that the Protestant population to be only 18 per cent in 1766. Parish cess figures in the Delgany vestry minutes (1667) record that a charge of £13 7s. 7d. was levied on Delgany and £13 2s. 10d. on Kilcoole (using nineteenth-century boundaries). If these charges were levied on a parish in proportion to the number of Protestants, this would suggest that Kilcoole and Delgany had roughly equal numbers of Protestants. However parish registers, by contrast, do indicate that Kilcoole had a greater Protestant population than did Delgany in the 1660s. Almost 30 per cent of all baptisms and burials between 1666 and 1774 were of people living in Kilcoole whereas Delgany only had 23 per cent of baptisms and burials. This fact alone suggests a higher Protestant population in Kilcoole.

34 *House of Lords journal (Ireland)*, iv, p. 370.

35 Summary Vol. Dublin Diocese (Religious Census) (N.A.I. M 2476 (i)).

36 See Gurrin, 'Populating a parish', p. 160 for a comment on the Dublin diocese Religious Census figures for the unions of Bray and Delgany and the parishes of Powerscourt and Newcastle.

37 Consider, for instance, the return for Shankill parish in the diocese of Dromore. Arthur Forde was appointed rector of the parish in 1748 and conducted a census of the parish during that year. In his returns to the House of Lords he cites the results of this census and provided townland breakdowns for 1766 and 1748 so that comparisons could be made (N.A.I. M 2476 (f)). This detailed return contrasts with the returns of many ministers who seem to have been greatly inconvenienced by the request.

38 T. O D. (Terence O Donnell), 'Parliamentary returns for the diocese of Raphoe, 1766' in *Donegal annual*, iii, no. 1, (1954–5), p. 74.

39 When the question of inquiring into religion in nineteenth-century censuses was being discussed, concerns were raised that the returns could be influenced by the bias of the enumerator, Malcolm P. A. Macourt, ' The religious inquiry in the Irish census of 1861', in *I.H.S.*, xxi, (1977–8), pp 169–70.

40 An omission rate of 14 per cent has been assumed when considering the 1669 Wicklow hearth-money roll. However, a local clergyman must surely have had a greater understanding of the population of his parish than a hearth-tax collector who was responsible for

collecting the tax over a far wider area.

41 No population figures are available for Bray in 1766 and thus the population density has not been calculated. It is probable that Bray parish was also more densely populated than Delgany in 1766.

42 *Notes made by S. Lane-Poole . . . hearth money, 1739* . . (N.L.I., Ms 7227).

43 Figures are available for the aggregate number of hearths in 1748 in each of the Rathdown and Newcastle parishes.

44 Dickson, Ó Gráda and Daultry, 'Hearth tax', p. 134.

45 Censuses were held every ten years from 1821 until 1911.

46 'The King's Commission to the Commisioners', in *First report of the commissioners of public instruction, Ireland*, iii, [C45], H.C. 1835, iii, 1.

47 Malcolm P. A. Macourt, 'The religious inquiry in the Irish census of 1861', in *I.H.S.*, xxi, (1977–8), p. 169.

48 In many cases the priest or minister conducted a census for the commissioners as was the case for the Delgany union and Bray and Newcastle parishes.

49 Macourt, 'The religious inquiry in the Irish census of 1861', p. 170.

50 Fraser, *General view of the agriculture . . . of the County Wicklow.*

51 Radcliff, *A report of the agriculture and livestock of the County of Wicklow.*

52 Joseph Lee, 'On the accuracy of the pre-Famine Irish Censuses' in J. M. Goldstrom and L. A. Clarkson (ed.), *Irish population, economy and society* (Oxford, 1981), pp 37–56.

53 *Public instruction, Ireland*, p. 96b.

54 *Public instruction, Ireland*, p. 112b.

55 *Public instruction, Ireland*, p. 112b.

56 Lee, 'On the accuracy of the pre-Famine Irish Censuses', p. 56.

57 See Gurrin, 'Populating a parish', p. 50 for a graphical presentation of the information contained in table 13.

58 Comparing the ranking of the population of Bray, Delgany, Kilmacanoge, Kilcoole, Powerscourt and Newcastle produces Spearman rank correlation values (r_s) of 0.94 for the 1669 and 1739 estimates, 1.00 for the 1669 and 1748 estimates and 0.94 for the 1669 and 1766 values. The advance in Bray's population in the early part of the nineteenth century results in an r_s value of 0.54 for the 1669 and 1831 estimates.

59 For the purpose of this exercise the population of Bray in 1766 was estimated at 584. This estimate is calculated by applying the Bray proportion of the Bray union population in 1669 (c. 35.5 per cent) to the 1766 census figure of 1,645.

60 Note that the 1766 Religious Census for the Bray union does not contain population figures for the individual parishes. It is possible, therefore, that one or two of the parishes in the union had proportionately more Protestants than Delgany.

FROM THE CRADLE TO THE GRAVE:
NATURAL POPULATION CHANGE IN
THE DELGANY UNION, 1666–1779

1 See E. A. Wrigley and R. S. Schofield, *The population history of England 1541–1871: a reconstruction*, (Cambridge, 1981) and Michael Drake (ed.), *Population studies from parish registers. A selection of readings from Local Population Studies*, (Derbyshire, 1982) for examples of the advanced nature of British demographic study.

2   Valerie Morgan, 'A case study of
    population change over two
    centuries: Blaris, Lisburn
    1661–1848' in *Irish Economic and
    Social History*, iii, (1976), pp 5–16;
    Valerie Morgan, 'The Church of
    Ireland registers of St Patrick's,
    Coleraine as a source for the study
    of a local pre-famine population' in
    Ulster Folklife, xix, (1973), pp 56–67;
    Valerie Morgan, 'Mortality in
    Magherafelt, County Derry, in the
    early eighteenth century' in *I.H.S.*,
    xix, (1974), pp 125–135; William
    Macafee, 'The colonisation of the
    Maghera region of South Derry
    during the seventeenth and
    eighteenth centuries' in *Ulster
    Folklife*, xxiii (1977), pp 70–91;
    William Macafee and Valerie
    Morgan, ' Historical revision xxi:
    Mortality in Magherafelt, County
    Derry, in the early eighteenth
    century reappraised' in *I.H.S.*, xxiii
    (1983), pp. 50–60.
3   Raymond Refaussé, 'Church
    records' in William Nolan and
    Anngret Simms (eds.), *Irish Towns. A
    guide to sources*, (Dublin, 1998), p.
    137; John Grenham, *Tracing your
    Irish ancestors*, (Dublin, 1992), p. 32.
    Also, see section XLVI of the 46th
    Canon from the Constitutions and
    Canons Ecclesiastical of the Irish
    Church which is replicated in
    Raymond Refaussé, 'The records
    of the Church of Ireland' in James
    G. Ryan (ed.), *Irish Church Records
    their history, availability and use in
    family and local history research*,
    (Dublin, 1992), p. 43.
4   Hull, *The economic writings of Sir
    William Petty*, i p. 210.
5   Bray parish records, (R.C.B. Lib.,
    Collection p. 580).
6   Powerscourt parish records,
    (R.C.B. Lib., Collection p. 109).
7   *D.P.R.1.*

8   *Liber Baptizatorum et
    Matrimoniorum*. Holy Redeemer
    church, Bray, Roman Catholic
    records – in local custody. Brian
    Mitchell, *A guide to Irish parish
    registers*, (Baltimore, 1988), p. 132
    incorrectly states that Bray records
    commence in 1800.
9   Enniskerry Roman Catholic parish
    registers available on microfilm in
    N.L.I., p 6478.
10 Mitchell, *A guide to Irish parish
    registers*, pp 132–4. Bray records
    commenced in 1792.
11 For a detailed analysis of Church of
    Ireland records in the half-barony
    of Rathdown (Wicklow) as a
    source for population change see
    Brian Gurrin, 'An identification of
    some of the sources for Population
    levels and population changes in
    the half-barony of Rathdown
    (Wicklow) in the 18th & 19th
    century and the impacts of
    population change on standard of
    livings in the region', 1998, pp
    45–47; copy with author.
12 Drake, *Population studies from parish
    registers*, pp v–xxv.
13 See Maureen Wall, *The penal laws*,
    1691–1760, (Dublin, 1976).
14   Refaussé, 'Church records', p. 137.
15 Methodist ministers did not baptise
    until the 1830s. Before this
    Methodist children were baptised
    in Church of Ireland churches;
    Refaussé, 'Church records', p. 137.
16 Drake, *Population studies from parish
    registers*, pp viii–ix.
17 The earliest Powerscourt records
    were transcribed in 1732; see A. E.
    Stokes, *The parish of Powerscourt*,
    (1963), p. 12.
18 Gurrin, 'Populating a parish',
    pp 61–7.
19 Gurrin, 'Populating a parish', p. 181.
20 Years of distress have principally
    been determined from Wilde's table

of famines in E. Margaret Crawford
(ed.), 'William Wilde's table of Irish
famines' in E.M. Crawford (ed.),
*Famine: the Irish experience,
900–1900*, (Edinburgh, 1989), pp
1–30 and from David Dickson,
'The gap in famines: a useful
myth?' in Crawford, *Famine: the
Irish experience 900–1900*, pp 96–111.

21　Dickson, 'The gap in famines' p. 99.

22　Dickson, 'The gap in famines' p. 99.

23　*D. V.B.1.* See vestry meetings held 3
September 1725 and 30 March
1730. At the 1725 meeting there
were eleven on the list but by 1730
the list had grown to fourteen.

24　Dickson, 'The gap in famines',
p. 100 and p. 105.

25　Dickson, 'The gap in famines' p.
102.

26　1746 was a year of high Dublin
wheat prices, Dickson, 'The gap in
famines' p. 99.

27　Dickson, 'The gap in famines', p.
104.

28　Powerscourt graph is available in
Gurrin, 'Populating a parish',
p. 181.

29　See Drake, *Population studies from
parish registers* and Kussmaul, *A
general view of the rural economy of
England*, pp 14–18.

30　L. Bradley, ' An inquiry into
seasonality in baptisms, marriages
and burials. Part 3. Burial
seasonality' in Drake, *Population
studies from parish registers*, p. 87.

31　L. Bradley, ' An enquiry into
seasonality in baptisms, marriages
and burials. Part 2. Baptism
seasonality' in Drake, *Population
studies from parish registers*, p. 23.

32　Caroline Brettell, *Men who migrate,
women who wait. Population and
history in a Portuguese parish*, (New
Jersey, 1986), p. 95.

33　Reliable birth-baptism interval
information does not become

available for the Delgany area until
1819. Of the 290 baptisms between
3 October 1819 and 29 October
1826 for which the birth-baptism
interval is known, the months with
the largest intervals are August
(20.5 days), November (20 days),
March (17.5 days) and December
(16 days). None of these intervals
are excessively long and do not
differ substantially from the average
figure of 15 days (intervals greater
than 90 days not included when
calculating these figures).
Furthermore, the intervals for
September and October, prime
harvest months, are only 12 days
and 15.5 days respectively.

34　Harvest wage rates in north-east
Wicklow are given in the *First
report from the commissioners for
inquiring into the condition of the poor
in Ireland – appendix D containing
baronial examinations relative to
earnings of labourers, cottier tenants,
employment of women and children,
expenditure; and supplement containing
answers to questions 1 to 12, circulated
by the commissioners*, Supplement to
appendix D, pp 149–50, H.C. 1836
(36), xxxi, part 4. As can be seen in
this report, wages increased by up
to 50 per cent or more for the
duration of the harvest. For
instance, Arthur Jones stated that in
Delgany, Kilmacanoge and Kilcoole
'Wages are 10*d.* and 1*s.* per day;
with diet 6*d.* per day; during
harvest from 1*s.* 6*d.* to 2*s.* and 2*s.* 6*d*
per day.', p. 150.

35　Gurrin, 'Populating a parish', pp
85–7.

36　January was also a common month
for burials between 1700 and 1719.

37　Gurrin, 'Populating a parish',
pp 85–7.

38　Gurrin, 'Populating a parish',
pp 88–9.

THE RHYTHMS OF THE HOME:
FAMILY LIFE IN THE DELGANY
UNION, 1666–1779

1   Arthur Young, *A tour in Ireland . . .
    in the years 1776, 1777 and 1778*, ed.
    Constantia Maxwell (Cambridge,
    1925), pp 29–30.
2   Ten of the baptisms recorded
    between 1666–1779 in the Delgany
    union are certainly of children
    born out of wedlock. Another 14
    baptisms are of children against
    which no father's name is recorded
    which may indicate that the father
    was unknown.
3   On average there were 1.94
    marriages recorded per year
    between 1666 and 1779.
4   Thomas Hammond and Letice
    Keightly, who married in Delgany
    on 19 April 1752, appear to have
    settled in the parish because they
    had a child baptised on 19
    February 1753.
5   The forty-eight brides for which
    age of marriage figures can be
    calculated are listed in Gurrin,
    'Populating a parish', pp 183–5.
6   The complete data from which the
    decade-by-decade average age of
    marriage figures have been
    calculated is shown in Gurrin,
    'Populating a parish', pp 186–8.
7   *D.P.R.1*, Elizabeth Bryan married
    on 9 June 1754 and Anne Grundy
    married on 2 February 1757.
8   John Demos, *A little commonwealth
    Family life in Plymouth Colony*,
    (Oxford, 1970), pp 66–7.
9   *D.P.R.1*, Jarvis Boswell married
    Mary Darbishire on 19 January
    1675 and their son, John, was
    baptised on 4 February 1696.
10 *D.P.R.1*, Mary Boswell was buried
    on 25 May 1696. Boswell's eldest
    child, Mary, was baptised on 23
    August 1691.

11 *D.P.R.1*, Gervas Boswell married
    Grace Hornby on 12 August 1697.
    They had a son, John, baptised on
    24 November 1698 and a daughter
    Sarah was baptised on 29
    September 1715.
12 *D.P.R.1*, John, son of Jervis and
    Mary Boswell, was buried on 24
    June 1696. John, son to Jervis and
    Grace Boswell was baptised on 24
    November 1698.
13 Gurrin, 'Populating a parish', pp
    189–91.
14 Intervals of five years or more
    between marriage and the baptism
    of the couples first child are
    exceptional and are more likely a
    result of poor registration or other
    factors.
15 The calculation of the marriage-
    first birth interval for the various
    periods are shown in Gurrin,
    'Populating a parish', pp 193–7.
16 A total of 291 marriages were
    recorded in the Delgany registers
    between 1666 and 1819.
17 Kussmaul, *A general view of the rural
    economy of England*, pp 14–45.
18 Harvest wage rates in north-east
    Wicklow are given in the *First
    report from the commissioners for
    inquiring into the condition of the poor
    in Ireland – appendix D containing
    baronial examinations relative to
    earnings of labourers, cottier tenants,
    employment of women and children,
    expenditure; and supplement containing
    answers to questions 1 to 12, circulated
    by the commissioners*, Supplement to
    appendix D, pp 149–50, H.C. 1836
    (36), xxxi, part 4. As can be seen,
    wages increased by up to 50 per
    cent or more for the duration of
    the harvest.
19 Kussmaul, *A general view of the rural
    economy of England*, p. 15.
20 Kussmaul, *A general view of the rural
    economy of England*, p. 15.

21 Kussmaul, *A general view of the rural economy of England,* pp 17–22.

22 In grain producing regions in pre-Industrial Revolution days wages increased to high levels during the harvest time. That Powerscourt was predominantly pasture can be seen from the wages rates reported by the *First report from the commissioners for inquiring into the condition of the poor in Ireland – appendix D,* Supplement, 1836 (36), xxxi, part 4. In Delgany, Kilcoole and Kilmacanoge 'wages are 10*d.* and 1*s.* per day; with diet 6*d.* per day; during harvest from 1*s.* 6*d.* to 2*s.* and 2*s.* 6*d.* per day' (p. 150) whereas in Powerscourt there was no wage increase during autumn – '1*s.* per day in summer, 10*d.* in winter, without diet; and 6*d.* with diet' (p. 150).

23 Of the 41 houses recorded in Bray parish in the 1669 hearth-money roll, 14 were located in Great Bray (Gurrin, 'Populating a parish', pp 143–59). Also, of the 54 hearth-tax payers in Old Connaught parish in 1664, 10 lived in Little Bray town (Gurrin, 'Populating a parish', pp 139–42).

24 L. Bradley, ' An inquiry into seasonality in baptisms, marriages and burials. Part 1. Marriage seasonality' in Drake, *Population studies from parish registers,* p. 9.

25 The details of these fifty-four marriages including the dates of the marriage and of Easter are listed in Gurrin, 'Populating a parish', pp 219–222.

26 Kussmaul, *A general view of the rural economy of England,* p. 21.

27 Gurrin, 'Populating a parish', p. 218.

28 *D.P.R.1,* John Bunn was baptised on 5 January 1757 and James Bunn was baptised on 6 December 1757.

29 See preceding footnote. *D.P.R.1,* Other children to James and Elizabeth Bunn were Mary

baptised on 11 April 1760, Elizabeth baptised on 24 March 1761, Thomas (Bunne) baptised on 25 May 1762, Samuel baptised on May 1763, Molly baptised on 29 July 1764, Joseph baptised on 4 August 1765, William baptised on 7 June 1767, Catharine baptised on 18 July 1769, Sophia and Jane baptised on 4 September 1770, Sarah baptised on 16 June 1773 and Joseph baptised on 19 July 1775.

30 *D.P.R.1,* Mary buried 13 April 1760, aged two days, Joseph buried 20 July 1767, aged one year eleven months, William buried 25 April 1768, aged 10 months and Joseph buried 1 August 1775 aged two weeks.

31 Gurrin, 'Populating a parish', pp 189–91.

32 Gurrin, 'Populating a parish', p. 112.

33 See Gurrin, 'Populating a parish', pp 115–6 and pp 198–200 for an explanation of the method used to calculate Protestant estimates for 1739 and 1748.

34 D. E. C. Eversley, 'A survey of population in an area of Worcestershire from 1600 to 1850 on the basis of parish registers' in D. V. Glass and D. E. C. Eversley (eds.), *Population in history, essays in historical demography,* (London, 1965), p. 408.

35 I have deliberately excluded the burial rate of 65.92 per thousand in Worcestershire between 1725–9 as this was exceptional.

36 Brian J Cantwell, *Memorials of the dead – N. E. Wicklow,* (1971–1974), section 11.

37 Cantwell, *Memorials of . . . N. E. Wicklow,* section 11, p. 1 (unnumbered).

38 Cantwell, *Memorials of . . . N. E. Wicklow,* section 11, p. 6 (unnumbered).

39 John Ferrar, *A view of ancient and modern Dublin, with its improvements*

to the year *1796. To which is added a tour to Bellevue, in the county of Wicklow, the seat of Peter La Touche Esq;*, (Dublin, 1796), p. 96.

40 *D. V.B.1.* At a vestry meeting held on 8 April 1751 it was decided that no more than sixteen names were to be included on the parish poor list, of whom twelve had to be Protestants.

41 Listing of the parish poor for 1716 is contained in the *D. V.B.1.*

42 'A trip through part of the County of Wicklow, in July, 1791' in *Walker's Hibernian magazine: or compendium of entertaining knowledge, for April, 1793,* (1793), pp 307–11.

43 'A trip through part of the County of Wicklow, in July, 1791', p. 310.

44 The method used to determine infant mortality is outlined in Gurrin, 'Populating a parish', pp 121–2.

45 See Gurrin, 'Populating a parish', pp 124–5 for an annual breakdown of infant mortality as a proportion of total deaths between 1737 and 1760.

46 Jo[seph] Fox of Newtownmount-kennedy paid hearth-money in 1669.

47 *D.P.R.1,* John Fox was baptised on 16 February 1697.

48 See Gurrin, 'Populating a parish', pp 206–17 for a listing of all of the 590 surnames occurring in the Delgany union baptism and burial records between 1666 and 1777.